Turkey Hunting
with Gerry Blair
Blair

by Gerry Blair

Copyright 1991 by Krause Publications

**Published by
Krause Publications, Inc.
700 E. State Street
Iola, WI 54990
Telephone: 715/445-2214**

Library of Congress Catalog Number : 90-63915
International Standard Book Number : 0-87341-160-9

Printed in the United States of America

FOREWORD

I have a temptation to use this space to individually thank each and every one of the Turkey Hunter readers (about 70,000) for the fine support they have offered to my writing, and to my editorship, since the magazine was birthed in March of 1984. You will likely be happy to hear I have resisted that temptation. Let me say, however, that you know who you are. Your support is appreciated. Permit me, instead, to call the names of a few folks who have substantially contributed to my development as a writer, an editor, and as a turkey hunter.

Jim Mohr, has offered trust and support. Pat Klug, Book Manager for Krause Publications, has done the same. All of the folks at Krause Publications, from proof reading to layout, have worked very hard to make me look a lot better than I ever hope to be.

My many years as editor of Turkey Hunter Magazine have exposed me to some of the finest folks in the world. All of them good hunters and all are fine gentlemen. Folks like Jim Clay of Perfection Calls, Kelly Cooper of Kelly Kallers, Neil (Gobbler) Cost, Ray Eye, Bill Harper, Brad Harris of Lohman Manufacturing, Allen Jenkins of Lynch Calls, Dick Kirby of Quaker Boy, Frank Piper of Penn's Woods, Preston Pittman of Preston Pittman Game Calls, Roger Raisch, Eddie Salter of Eddie Salter Calls, Gene Smith Editor of Turkey Call and Lovett Williams of Real Turkeys. My life has been enriched by knowing you all.

I also wish to recognize a young man who has been a pleasant companion on many hunts for turkey, mule deer, elk and antelope. Larry Gates of Congress, Arizona is a friend in every sense of the word.

I wish to thank the lady who has shared my successes and failures for nearly forty years. Ann Coveny Blair encouraged me to write this book even though she knows from past experience how my personality changes when I shift to my book writing mode. I become compulsive and non-communicative. My mind spends a good deal of time in far away places. I am, in short, a real dog (even more so than usual). She gives the word wife a good name.

Finally, I wish to thank all who generously contributed expertise and advice. Most have been mentioned already. They deserve credit for much that is good in this book.

ABOUT THE AUTHOR

Gerry Blair retired from a 25 year law enforcement career in 1976 to pursue a lifelong journalistic goal. Since that time Blair has written five books and has authored more than 500 freelance articles. Most of his work is illustrated with his own photography, much of it showing wildlife in natural settings.

The Flagstaff, Arizona resident is editor of Turkey Hunter Magazine, associate editor of Trapper & Predator Caller, and is a contributing editor of Rock & Gem. Most of his time, he admits, is spent hunting, writing about hunting, or talking about hunting. A tough life, he says ruefully, but someone has to do it.

TABLE OF CONTENTS

IN THE BEGINNING ......
CHAPTER ONE

It took nature many millions of years to produce and fine tune the bird we know as the wild turkey. Modern man was more efficient in his (and her) efforts to eradicate the species common to much of the United States. There were an estimated ten million turkeys in the "new world" when the gang of 102 Englanders established the first permanent colony at Plymouth, Massachusetts in 1620. Two hundred and thirty one years later the last of the big birds was sighted in Massachusetts near Mount Tom. Within the next fifty years, less than three centuries after settlement, the magnificent wild turkey was gone or going in most of its historic range.

Modern man knows little about the turkeys of pre-history. The few facts available have been assembled from scant evidence. A fragment of fossil bone in most instances, and rarely, a complete or nearly complete fossil skeleton. This evidence from a time long past leaves little doubt that a relative of the American wild turkey lived in North America during ancient times. That turkey, zoologists speculate, was somewhat similar in form to the five subspecies of *Meleagris gallopavo* presently found in North America.

Meleagris Gallopavo is the common turkey of North America. That bird, and his uncommon cousin of southern Mexico and adjoining parts of central America (*Meleagris ocellata*) are the sole survivors of that turkey of ancient times.

The Aztec Indians of Southern Mexico domesticated the turkey. This pottery whistle was obviously turkey inspired.

7

We know much about the turkey that lived in the more modern part of prehistory. The Indians of North America had a long and beneficial relationship with the wild turkey, an interaction that extended back far beyond the time when the first non-Indians appeared in North America about five hundred years ago. It is believed that the Aztec Indians of southern Mexico domesticated *Meleagris gallopavo* (now extinct) about the time that Christ was born.

Some scientists suggest that the Goulds and the Merriams may be nothing more than isolated strains of the extinct turkey of southern Mexico. Ancient Indians, they postulate, were nomadic. Many maintained somewhat sophisticated trade routes that took them to many parts of northern Mexico and the southwestern United States. It is certainly possible they could have transported tamed turkeys to the mountain island habitat found in both areas. Separation from the mother stock for many hundreds of years could have caused the birds to develop the physical characteristics that permit them to be identified as a sub-species.

The tamed turkeys of the Aztecs were taken to Spain about 1519 and travelled to England about 1541. Some of those domesticated birds were returned to North America when the pilgrims colonized about eighty years later.

Those domesticated turkeys were the progenitors of the many millions of domestic turkeys of diverse strains found today. Selective breeding has caused strains such as the Bronze, White Holland, Bourbon Red, Black, Slate and the Narragansett. All are descendants of that original Aztec race.

Available evidence suggests that the wild turkey, and the tamed strains of the wild turkey, was an important food for the Indian. The old time hunting technique was probably similar to the technique modern archers use to outwit North America's biggest game bird. The hunter would find an area where the turkey came to feed or water. Or he would find a travelway between the roosting area and the feeding area and would hide out until a turkey came close enough to be killed.

Many modern hunters are able to duplicate many parts of the turkey vocabulary using their natural voice, the edge of a leaf or a call made from the wing bones of a wild turkey hen. It is reasonable to believe that some of the Indian hunters, maybe even most, had mastered basic turkey calling skills.

The bow and arrow used by these ancient hunters was considerably less sophisticated than modern archery equipment. The Indians had no compound bows, no recurves, no sight pins and no arrows made of perfectly balanced aluminum tubing. The Indian bow was made of wood and was sometimes backed with rawhide or shaved bone. The Indian bow was short and was sometimes fire hardened to provide strength.

Indian arrow shafts were often made of fire hardened wood and were usually tipped with stone heads knapped from agate, jasper, chert or obsidian. One type of arrowhead, serrated and considerably smaller than the points used for big game hunting or for war, has come to be called a "bird point".

Some small arrowheads knapped by southwestern Indians have come to be called "bird points".

Some southwestern Indians modified a wild turkey spur for use as an arrow point.

Arrowheads have been recovered from burials that were made of a more exotic material, the spur taken from the leg of a mature male turkey. The hollow spur was removed from the rear of each lower leg and was trued by abrading it with a piece of sandstone or other natural abrasive. The modified spur was then attached to the end of the arrow shaft using a melted mastic made from the gum of the pinion pine tree.

The Indians of pre-history used the wild turkey mainly for food but other parts were not wasted. Wild turkey wing feathers were trimmed and attached to arrow shafts with the same gum glue to serve as a fletching. Other feathers were sewn into the clothing to serve as a decoration. The awl used for the sewing, much of the time, was made from a splinter of wild turkey bone.

Turkey feathers were sometimes sewn to a tanned leather backing to construct a blanket or ceremonial robe of great beauty and great value. With imagination one can visualize the splendent play of color as the sunlight, or the firelight, played across the handsome iridescence of the feathers.

One Rocky Mountain tribe, the Crows, made a ceremonial whistle from the leg bone of a wild turkey. Such a whistle, historians report, was highly prized.

Prehistory pottery recovered from burials show that the turkey image was a popular subject, particularly in plates, bowls and pots used for ceremonial purposes. The images appeared as a great variety of stylized drawings.

The pueblo dwellers of the Southwest painted stylized interpretations of the turkey onto ceremonial pottery.

The rock pickings archaeologists call petroglyphs, and the less common paintings called pictographs, also showed a fair number of turkey images.

The non-Indians who came to the new world shared the Indian taste for turkey. It has been mentioned that the early Englanders came to our shores carrying caged specimens of domestic turkeys. Hundreds of years of selective breeding followed and produced the mega-birds (some weighing as much as 65 pounds) that now decorate a good many Thanksgiving Day tables.

Those pilgrims who made the one way trip to the new world soon developed a taste for the wild turkey as well. Turkey hunting for the table became a popular pastime. Turkey hunting for the market became an art form. Commercial hunters developed ways to take the greatest amount of meat using the least amount of powder and shot (and effort). Turkey "lining" was a much used tactic. Bait lines of corn were laid out in a line that might extend for fifty feet. In good turkey country (and there was a lot of it then) the line would be well attended in short order. The "hunter," hidden in his blind, would wait until turkeys were crowded shoulder to shoulder along the line, each with his or her head down to gobble as much of the corn as possible. The shooter would then make a sound that would cause the turkeys to raise their heads to investigate. A split second later the blast of the market gun, a ten gauge, would rape the forest stillness and the line of turkeys, or most of them, would fall flopping.

Wild turkey was a staple in many frontier meat markets. And the turkey meat was cheap. John James Audubon, writing of America during the 1800's, reported that a ten pound bird might be priced at three pence. A first class bird, a gobbler that tipped the scales to 25 pounds, might cost a quarter of a dollar. At a penny a pound, even by frontier standards, turkey was a bargain.

Turkeys were present in great flocks in frontier America and were a staple of early day meat markets.

The demand for wild turkey meat, and the efficiency of the market hunters, played an important part in the extirpation of the turkey from much of his historic range. Other factors contributed. The clear cutting of vast tracts of forest land to make way for residences, cities and agriculture certainly hastened the demise of the wild turkey. It is possible that avian diseases introduced by the small flocks of domesticated turkeys might have also contributed.

Even though turkey numbers diminished no one was worried. There seemed to be an inexhaustible supply of the big black birds. A Massachusetts settler reported the sighting of more than a thousand birds during the course of a half day hunt that took place in 1620. A South Carolina hunter claimed he sighted a single flock that contained more than 500 wild turkeys.

In spite of the numbers present, even that vast resource could not withstand the twin threats of market hunting and habitat loss.

The turkey was gone from much of his historic range in a surprisingly short time. The turkey was gone from Massachusetts by 1851, gone from Ohio by 1880 and gone from Michigan by 1881. Gone gone gone. The last half of the past century, and the first half of the current century, were the wild turkeys' darkest days. The blood stirring sound of the spring gobble was gone, or nearly gone, from nearly every part of the original 39 state range. The wild turkey, simply stated, was well on the way to join the passenger pigeon as a shameful monument to the national appetite and the greed of those who hunted to satisfy that appetite.

Finally a dim light appeared in the almost dark tunnel. The congress passed a law (the Pittman-Robertson Act of 1937) that legislated a hunter tax. Outdoorsmen and women paid a tax on every gun, on every shell and on many other items of outdoor equipment. The money collected was set aside for aid to wildlife, particularly for wildlife restoration. That money, coupled with concern and an increasing knowledge of the biologic and habitat needs of the wild turkey, set the stage for a remarkable wild turkey comeback.

By 1958 the restocking of the wild turkey had caused the gobble to return to spring woods that had been silent for a hundred years. County by county and state by state, as the mechanics of cannon netting and transplantation became refined, the big birds prospered. And as populations permitted, the hunters who had borne the main part of the cost of the restoration were allowed to go to the woods to harvest surplus birds.

Currently the wild turkey is present in every U.S. state except Alaska. The wild turkey is present in Canada and in Mexico. And almost every one of those areas has huntable populations. Once again hunters can go to the spring or fall woods to match wits with the wariest of the game birds. Good game management, coupled with wise use of habitat, should keep the big birds healthy and huntable for generations to come.

TAKING A LOOK AT TURKEY TYPES
CHAPTER TWO

Wildlife biologists and zoologists have identified two species of the wild turkey, *Meleagris gallopavo* and *Meleagris ocellata.* The best known, and the most common, is the big bird of North America called *Meleagris gallopavo.* That turkey has been categorized into five living sub-species. The sub-species of gallopavo differ only slightly in appearance, the obvious difference being in the amount of white present at the tail tips and on the wing bars. The three western sub-species, generally speaking, are shorter of leg and a bit more stocky than the two eastern sub-species.

In areas where the range of one sub-species, or race, of the wild turkey overlaps the range of a different sub-species interbreeding can (and usually does) take place. This interbreeding produces a hybrid strain that muddies the already tenuous elements of identification. And although this hybridization interests biologists and some hunters, the turkeys accept the fact without comment. Every race of turkey will readily mate with others of the wild turkey family (within the same species) if the opportunity is presented. Wild turkeys of every sub-species of gallopavo will passionately mate with the fatso's of domestic turkeydom just as readily.

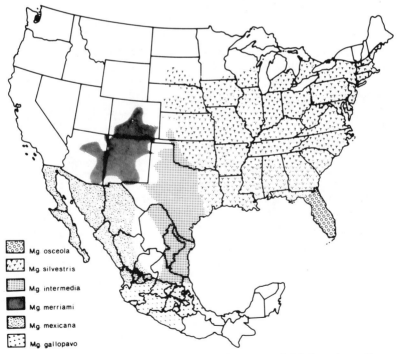

Mg osceola

Mg silvestris

Mg intermedia

Mg merriami

Mg mexicana

Mg gallopavo

Distribution chart showing original range of Meleagris gallopavo sub-species.

The wild turkey found in northern Florida is an example of inter-breeding between sub-species. The Florida turkey, also called the Osceola, is native to southern Florida. The eastern sub-species is native to northern Florida. Where the ranges overlap the turkeys have bred to produce a strain that is neither pure Osceola or Eastern, but is instead a mixture of each.

The transplantation of birds to historic and non-historic range has caused a further mixing. In certain parts of California Rio Grande turkeys, Easterns and Merriams have been released. The turkeys got together with considerable gusto (it's that California life style) to produce a colony of turkey that has come to be called the "California Turkey". It is, in actuality, nothing more and nothing less than a hybrid turkey who traces ancestry to the three sub-species introduced.

The five living sub-species of gallopavo are the Eastern and the Osceola in the east and the Goulds, the Merriams and the Rio Grande in the west. The characteristics that identify the races, as has been mentioned, is subtle, limited in most instances to gradations of color. The identification of the sub- species, much of the time is dependent on where that turkey happens to live. Put another way, when it comes right down to the nitty and the gritty, identification is mainly geographic. A wild turkey that lives (or dies) in Pennsylvania is almost always considered to be of the Eastern race regardless of color aberrations that may be noticed.

Color aberration is sometimes found in every sub-species of gallopavo. Missouri hunter Wayne Gendron killed a color aberrant Eastern wild turkey in the Missouri Ozarks in 1964 that showed a reddish aberration. The bird had body feathers that were a burnt orange color. The wing feathers were nearly snow white. The big bird (21 pounds, 10" beard and 1 1/8" spurs) was examined by a biologist from the Missouri Conservation Commission who postulated the wild bird had an ancestor who may have been an albino.

Turkey biologist Lovett Williams wrote on color aberration in the wild turkey in an article published in the September 1987 issue of *Turkey Hunter* magazine. Dr. Williams said he has seen a red (erythristic) adult gobbler in southern Mississippi and a red and white adult gobbler in Nassau County Florida. "It should not be necessary to point out", Dr. Williams commented, "that the wild turkey is capable of color aberrancy independent of any supposed contamination by domestic strains".

Much has been made in some literature about the supposed "contamination" of the pure wild turkey stock with genes from the domestic turkey. It is a fact that some early restocking efforts in parts of the east saw pen raised birds (cross-bred birds from wild and domestic stock) released to the wild. These efforts were failures. The wild turkey, it seemed, needed every element of his wildness to survive.

It is likely that some did survive to breed with pure wild stock, however, and it is just as likely that in some parts of the east these mixed blood birds are running wild and free. If the premise that domestic genes doom a wild bird is correct, those birds are doomed. They will be genetically inferior to the wild strain and will eventually perish.

Lovett Williams reports on an experiment he conducted with mixed blood birds in his excellent "The Book of the Wild Turkey" (Real Turkeys, 2201 Southeast 41st Avenue, Gainesville, FL 32601). Dr. Williams reared turkeys from wild eggs and crossed those turkeys with domestic turkeys. The crossbreeding continued until a bird that was 7/8ths wild was produced. Even then these mostly wild birds showed characteristics of the domestic strain, larger heads, shorter legs and variations in tail and wing color.

In another experiment four birds that were 3/4 wild stock and 1/4 domestic stock were released to the wild in good turkey habitat in northern Florida. All were wearing radio transmitters to track their movement. Within one month all were dead of predation. A bobcat took two and birds of prey took the other two.

Meleagris gallopavo silvestris, commonly called the Eastern turkey, is the bird of the east, some parts of the midwest, and the south. The Eastern turkey is mainly a bird of the hardwood forests, an area that produces much in the way of mast crops. The subspecies designator "silvestris", as a point of information, translates to woodlands. The Eastern bird is essentially a woodlands dweller.

Capture and release programs have returned the Eastern turkey to many parts of its historic range. Ohio DNR Photo.

Much of the Eastern range is characterized by hardwoods interrupted by farmland. This hardwood-farmland habitat offers an attractive mix to the wild turkey. Pennsylvania, one of the pioneer states in the restocking of the wild turkey, has a high population of Easterns. So does the neighboring State of New York.

Missouri, another advocate of turkey capture and transfer technology, has a high number of Easterns and is known nation wide for the turkey hunting opportunities offered to both resident and nonresident hunters.

Many of the southern states, Alabama, and Mississippi come immediately to mind, are well turkied.

All states mentioned, as well as many other states, are prime Eastern turkey habitat and offer quality turkey hunting opportunities.

The appearance of the typical Eastern turkey is somewhat distinctive. The tail tips can be chocolate or buff. The primary wing feathers are barred with the white bars divided by a black bar of similar width.

Meleagris gallopavo osceola, the Florida turkey, is similar to the Eastern in coloration although the barring of the wing feathers is slightly different. In the Osceola black predominates as a wing color.

The Ocellated turkey is clothed in feathers of unusual beauty.

The range of the Osceola turkey (named to honor a 19th century Indian chief of the Seminole tribe) is limited to the peninsula of Florida. Other areas of Florida contain wild turkeys but those birds are either Easterns or are hybrids produced by the inter-breeding of the Eastern and the Osceola. Of all the sub-species the Osceola is the most restricted in range. Hunters who hope to take an Osceola must travel to South Florida to do so.

The Rio Grande brand wild turkey (*Meleagris gallopavo intermedia*) could almost be called the Texas turkey with considerable accuracy. The State of Texas has a hell of a lot (and maybe more) of Rio Grande turkeys. Western Oklahoma has some Rio's and so does southern Kansas. A small colony of Rios hang out in southeastern New Mexico. South of the border, in northeastern Mexico, Rio Grande turkeys can be found. And that is about it for the Rio Grande turkey.

In appearance the Rio Grande turkey reflects a compromise between eastern and western strains. That compromised appearance, apparently, influenced the zoologist who added the sub-species specific name intermedia.

The tail tips of the typical Rio Grande turkey can vary from yellowish-buff to a nearly pure white. Almost always the tail feather tips are lighter in color than those of either the Eastern or the Osceola, and are darker than either the Merriams or the Goulds.

Rio Grande turkeys do well on the hardwood/farm field habitat found in southern Kansas.

Rio Grande range can and does vary. Much of the Texas habitat is composed of mesquite dotted rangeland. Groves of oak, locally called mottes, offer mast and roost sites. In southern Kansas the Rio habitat looks to be more Eastern in nature. Farmland alternates with hardwood ridges to form a habitat that looks typically Eastern. In Oklahoma much of the Rio Grande habitat is open farmland interrupted by tree lined waterways. The cottonwood trees along these waterways provide roost sites and provide cover. The Rio Grande brand turkey is an adaptable bird.

The Merriams is a migratory bird in much of its historic range, moving from high country to low country as snow deepens.

The Merriams turkey (*Meleagris gallopavo merriami*) is a bird that originally hung out mainly in the mountainous areas of Arizona and New Mexico. Restocking has caused the Merriams range to be considerably extended. The Black Hills of South Dakota now hold Merriams. So does the states of Wyoming, Montana, Idaho, Nebraska and a bunch of others.

Knowing of the Merriams origin, it is not surprising to learn that he is sometimes called the "mountain turkey". The Merriams (named to honor the zoologist C. Hart Merriam) is a bird that is tied to the ponderosa pine belt through much of his range, and to the foothills that surround such mountains. The Merriams is a migratory turkey in some parts of the range. Summer birds stay high on the mountain to take advantage of the ponderosa pine roost trees it favors, and to take advantage of a more dependable water and food supply. When the snow falls, when it becomes difficult for the mountain turkey to make a living at that high white altitude, the turkeys move down into the foothills, areas that sometimes support transition woodlands such as Gambel's oak and juniper. Biologists, using telemetry data, have verified a march of nearly sixty miles between summer and winter range.

Western turkeys, like this Merriams, have more white on the wing feathers than do either of the Eastern sub-species.

The Merriams turkey has nearly white tail feather tips, much more so than either of the eastern turkeys or of the Rio Grande. Not quite as white, in most instances, as those of the Goulds, but still mighty white.

The Goulds turkey (*Meleagris gallopavo mexicana*) is a close cousin to the Merriams in both appearance and range. The Gould's spends much of his time in the Sierra Madre Mountain range of Northern Mexico. Like the Merriams the Goulds migrate between summer and winter range as the weather dictates. The tail feather tips of the Goulds is more white than any of the other subspecies. The white band that borders the tail feathers is wider than in the Merriams. The rump patch of the Goulds, in most instances is less obvious than in the Merriams.

The Goulds turkey (a zoologist of that name described the Mexicana subspecies) is mainly a bird of northern Mexico. It should be mentioned that small remnant of populations remain in both Arizona and New Mexico. State and federal game management officials monitor those flocks carefully, hoping to return this handsome turkey to decent numbers within his historic range.

Alabama turkey hunter Eddie Salter hunted the Goulds turkey in the Sierra Madre Mountains in the spring of 1989. The Goulds, he says, is a turkey who is willing to cover a lot of ground to get to a willing hen. Eddie had a Gould travel from one mountain to another, crossing a steep canyon on the way, to get a close look at the critter that was making those seductive yelps, cutts and cackles.

The last turkey to be described is not a sub-species of gallopavo but is instead a separate species. *Meleagris ocellata* is the only other species of turkey to be found in the world. No sub-species have been identified. And as far as it is known, no ocellata has been domesticated.

Meleagris ocellata is found on the Yucatan Peninsula of Mexico and in the adjoining Central American countries of Guatemala and Belize. The Ocellated turkey may be the most beautiful bird in the world. Males and females are similarly colored. Each have a body color that is iridescent green with gold, copper, bronze and red flashes appearing as the light reflects. Neither sex carries a beard, as in gallopavo, but the male birds grow spurs. The bird is smaller than gallopavo. Males average about 12 pounds although some have been known to grow to 18 pounds. The Ocellated turkey is a bird of the jungle.

Taking a single sub-species of the wild turkey can be a challenge. Some hard hunters have compounded that challenge by establishing the grand slam of turkey hunting. The slam, technically, is the taking of one each of the four continental U.S. subspecies of the wild turkey, that is, the Eastern, the Osceola, the Rio Grande and the Merriams. An international slam includes the Goulds. A world slam brings in the Ocellated. There is not a consensus on terminology. To some hunters, to be significant, the taking of the turkeys must be accomplished within a single spring.

Few hunters can hope to spend the time or funds needed to complete any of the slams. Even so, hunters of moderate means have the opportunity to match wits with "the greatest gamebird" in their home state or in a neighboring state. To them, to most hunters, the taking of a single turkey by legal and sportsmanlike means, is a prideful event.

The taking of a wild turkey by legal and sportsmanlike means requires hunting skill and dedication.

THE SPRING HUNT
CHAPTER THREE

Turkey hunting is a two season sport. There are those who sincerely say they enjoy the fall hunt more than the spring hunt, or enjoy both equally. When you come across one of these yellow leaf advocates it is best to nod agreeably. Make a mental note, however, that this hunter is a compulsive liar. It is not possible for any hunt to surpass or equal the thrill found in matching wits with a white headed spring longbeard.

Fall hunting can be great. A hunter who feels his blood race as he rattles in a big necked whitetail will equally enjoy using a lost gobbler yelp, a coarse cluck or maybe even the seldom heard wildcat call to toll in an autumn longbeard. There is something about the frost and the fall woods that causes the hunting instinct to surface. Even so, as good as the fall hunt can be, it is a pathetically pale alternative to the spring hunt. If that were not so, how would one explain the fact that ordinarily sensible men and women leap from warm beds hours before first light to go to the spring woods to make a turkey scout? And stick to that same schedule day after day and week after week until they tag their turkey or the season ends? We are talking doctors, lawyers, judges, governors, presidents and day laborers. The wonderful affliction of spring turkey fever knows no economic or educational boundaries.

The spring hunt is a gobbler only hunt. Those paranoid longbeards of fall, skulking about the naked woods in small bachelor bands, have turned to vocal and aggressive romantics.

From a game management view many of those crazy in love spring gobblers are superfluous. Nature knew a lot about wild turkeys when she (or he) engineered this adaptable bird. Nature messed up, however, when it came to the turkey love life. About half of the turkey eggs hatched each summer are male turkeys. Turkey romance is not a situation where birds of opposite sex meet, date a few times, and then establish the shack-up some yuppies call a meaningful relationship. A tom turkey is interested in the hens purely and simply because of lust. He will gather as many as possible and mate with each of them repeatedly at the least encouragement. Each of those breedings is sufficient to fertilize the entire clutch of eggs. Every one of the remaining couplings, although neither hen nor gobbler is likely to admit it, is not creational but is instead recreational.

The first task of the spring turkey hunter is to locate a spring turkey. The second task is to definitely identify that turkey as a legal gobbler before the gun goes to the shoulder. A spring turkey gobbler is expendable. He can be harvested (killed graveyard dead) without seriously affecting the resource. Taking a turkey hen in the spring, however, removes that hen and the clutch of eggs she would have likely laid. That one mis-shot can take out the hen and all of her poults.

It is easy to determine sex when a tom and a hen are seen together but can be difficult when each is seen alone.

Telling the difference between a gobbler and a hen can be simple if the gobbler is swollen like a puffer, his head is a lust white, and his paintbrush beard drags the ground and the hen is right beside him as an insipid and unremarkable companion. Let that same hen sneak into the setup to confront a hunter whose blood is hot from the hunt with no companion to serve as point of reference, however, and the dis-similarity is less obvious.

It is good advice to watch for the beard. Even this somewhat sure means of identification carries an exception. Some hens have beards. The whiskers carried by these bearded ladies are seldom as grand as those grown by the gobbler. Hen beards are generally wispy and seldom exceed about eight inches. Having the beard does not seem to make the hen less attractive to the gobbler. That is not surprising. Some gobblers work themselves to such a lather that they might try to kiss a possum, or at the very least, fall desperately in love with a thin layer of plastic molded to somewhat resemble a turkey hen. Bearded hens normally nest, lay a clutch of eggs and hatch and raise the poults just as other hens do.

Even though the law mandates "a bearded bird" in many states, thus placing the bearded hen legally at risk, it is considered tacky to take a hen in the spring even though she is technically legal.

Here are sexual characteristics of hens and gobblers that might help you discover a legal target.

Adult hens are shorter and weigh less than an adult gobbler. When seen together the difference in size is apparent. The size disparity can be useful if a hen and a gobbler are together but may be less useful if the hen or the gobbler is alone with no point of reference to assist in identification.

The back of a gobblers neck is bare while a hen will show short feathers on the back of the neck. This feature is useful, generally, when the hunter is able to make an inspection through binoculars or if the birds are close.

Hens present a generally brown aspect while the gobblers are black and shiny. The breast feathers on the hen are brown tipped and those of a gobbler are black tipped.

No hunter, even though he may say that he can, will be able to immediately and positively identify sexuality each time he or she sees a turkey. It is important to know this and equally important to wait until you are absolutely sure before you pull the trigger. If evidence is not presented to your satisfaction let that turkey go. There will be others.

The most reliable distinguishing characteristics are head color (hens have blue heads, gobblers have pink or red on the side of the face), the presence of a beard (identifying a male bird 96- 98% of the time), the presence of spurs on the male bird, gobbling activity, and strutting (even though a very few hens may semi- strut at times).

A spring hunter is apt to encounter two types of male turkeys. A male turkey who is the young of the year (called a jake) resembles an adult male turkey in many aspects. He is nearly as large. He may strut and gobble. He has essentially the same coloration. His beard, however, is short and generally barely protrudes from his chest feathers. Button spurs also indicate a turkey that is the young of the year.

Hens have short feathers along back of head and neck and the head is a somewhat blue color.

A first year tom, called a jake, can be identified by a short beard, button spurs, and tail feathers of uneven length.

Some spring turkey hunters have set high personal goals and will not shoot the shot at a jake. Just as there are trophy deer hunters, there are those who take a special satisfaction in tying their tag to the leg of a super smart old longbeard. The National Wild Turkey Federation (P.O. Box 530, Edgefield, SC 29824), an organization dedicated to the welfare of the wild turkey, maintains a listing of wild turkey records. The following criteria governs scoring.

Measure the beard from where it grows from skin to the tip of the longest bristle.

Turkeys must be weighed to the closest ounce on scales certified accurate by the United States Department of Agriculture, on official scales of a governmental wildlife agency, or on accurate scales by a licensed guide or outfitter. Beard and spur measurements should be measured to closest 1/8". To obtain overall score multiply the right and left spur length by ten, the beard length by two, and add those totals to the weight in pounds and ounces (see the conversion chart). Measure the beard from the center point where it protrudes from the skin of the chest and then along the longest bristle. Measure each spur along a center line that follows the longest length, from the place of protrusion on the leg to the tip.

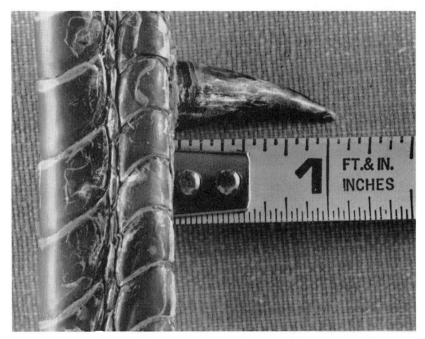

This is the wrong way to measure a spur. Measure at the top and along the curve to get accurate reading.

To be listed in the NWTF records the hunter must be a member of that organization. The measurements must be witnessed and verified by a second NWTF member. Other controls exist. To learn the total procedure, and to receive an entry form, contact the National Wild Turkey Federation, Wild Turkey Records, P.O. Box 530, Edgefield, SC 29824-0530 (803) 637-3106.

A listing of the first, second and third place record holders for the Ocellated turkey and for the five sub-species of *Meleagris gallopavo* follows.

CURRENT TURKEY RECORDS

EASTERN SUB-SPECIES

HUNTER	SCORE	DATE	STATE
BEST OVERALL EASTERN GOBBLER			
1. Gene Hostettler, Buffalo, MO	83.0000	5-1-89	MO
2. Donald McGrew, Fanklin OH	82.5000	5-8-85	OH
3. Larry D. Light, Hannibal, MO	80.7500	5-1-87	MO
HEAVIEST EASTERN GOBBLER			
1. W.V. Johnson, Cotter, AR	33.3750	4-2-87	AR
2. Craig A. Jessen, Hennepin, IL	33.2500	5-5-85	IL
3. Richard P. White, Maysville, GA	31.0625	3-23-87	GA
LONGEST BEARD ON EASTERN GOBBLER			
1. Kirk Files, Brinkley, AR	16.8750	3-23-85	AL
2. Buckey R. Garner, Cumming, GA	16.5000	4-3-86	GA
3. Brian T. Caton, Huntington, TN	14.7500	5-5-88	TN
LONGEST SPURS ON EASTERN GOBBLER			
1. Thomas R. Craig, Candor, NY	2.0000	5-8-80	NY
Donald Mcgrew, Franklin, OH	2.0000	5-8-85	OH
2. Arthur Drennan, Springfield, IL	1.8750	4-25-80	IL
Larry Fox, Birmingham, AL	1.8750		AL
David Street, Hattiesburg, MS	1.8750	3-24-86	MS
William Waterbury, Chandler, IN	1.8750	5-6-87	IN
3. Phillip Houser, Jacksonville, IL	1.8100	4-1-88	IL

MERRIAMS SUB-SPECIES

HUNTER	SCORE	DATE	STATE

BEST OVERALL MERRIAMS GOBBLER

HUNTER	SCORE	DATE	STATE
1. Russel Oakland, Sioux Falls, SD	73.2500	5-4-86	SD
2. Dennis Silgen, Thousand Oaks, CA	70.4400	4-26-85	CA
3. Loren Dellinger, Denver, CO	68.2500	4-9-87	SD

HEAVIEST BEARD ON MERRIAMS GOBBLER

HUNTER	SCORE	DATE	STATE
1. Elray Harper, Sidney, MT	28.0000	4-18-79	MT
2. Mike Caldarella, Anthony, NM	27.4375	4-20-87	NM
3. Russel Oakland, Sioux Falls, SD	26.2500	4-25-87	SD

LONGEST BEARD ON MERRIAMS GOBBLER

HUNTER	SCORE	DATE	STATE
1. Thomas M. Knight, Othello, WA	12.0000	4-?-78	WA
Frank Sack, Pierre, SD	12.0000	10-15-84	SD
2. Wm. McLaughlin, Redding, CA	11.5000	4-10-86	CA
3. Richard Farthing, Albany, OR	11.2500	3-30-85	CA
Larry Bennett, Grand Jct, CO	11.1250	5-10-86	CO
Corey Machanic, Rome, NY	11.1250	4-20-87	NM
Dennis Silgen, Thousand Oaks, CA	11.1250	4-16-85	CA

LONGEST SPURS ON MERRIAMS GOBBLERS

HUNTER	SCORE	DATE	STATE
1. Russel Oakland, Sioux Falls, SD	1.6250	5-4-86	SD
2. Richard Rossum, Rapid City, SD	1.5000	4-12-89	WY
3. Daniel Dexter, Duluth, NM	1.3750	4-6-85	SD
Paul Dickson, Shreveport, LA	1.3750	4-16-83	CO
Bo Hauer, Piedmont, SD	1.3750	4-16-75	SD
James Kohl, Cross Plains, WI	1.3750	4-4-89	WY
Dennis Silgen, Thousand Oaks, CA	1.3750	4-16-89	CA
Guy Tillett, Blackhawk, SD	1.3750	5-10-86	SD

RIO GRANDE SUB-SPECIES

HUNTER	SCORE	DATE	STATE
BEST OVERALL RIO GRANDE GOBBLER			
1. Anthony Brock, Ochopee, FL	79.0000	3-30-87	TX
2. Robert Blakeney, Dallas, TX	78.5000	4-13-86	TX
3. Jack Isaminger III, Dallas, TX	77.4375	4-9-88	TX
HEAVIEST RIO GRANDE GOBBLER			
1. Michael Fitzgerald, Ottawa, KS	28.5000	4-?-89	KS
2. Charles Kimball, Augusta, KS	27.0000	4-13-88	KS
3. J. Thompsom III, San Antonio, TX	26.6875	4-12-86	TX
LONGEST BEARD ON RIO GRANDE GOBBLER			
1. Charles Salter, Comanche, TX	15.0000	4-13-85	TX
2. Alvin Tisserand, Anderson, CA	14.8750	4-1-85	CA
3. W.S. Price Jr., Plano, TX	13.2500	4-3-88	TX
LONGEST SPURS ON RIO GRANDE GOBBLER			
1. Jack Kerr, Arlington, TX	2.0000	4-18-87	TX
2. Dave Burton, Redding, CA	1.8750	3-26-88	CA
3. Bob Bealtm, Elkins, WV	1.7500	4-17-87	TX
Robert Blakeney, Dallas, TX	1.7500	4-13-86	TX

OCELLATED TURKEY

HUNTER	WEIGHT	SPUR	SCORE	STATE
BEST OVERALL OCELLATED				
1. Starr Boykin, Mobile, AL	12.1250	2.1250	54.63	MX
2. J. Robert Boykin, Mobile, AL	11.7500	1.8750	50.50	MX
3. Bryan McCann, Marksville, LA	12.1250	1.8750	48.38	MX

BEST OVERALL ATYPICAL GOBBLER
(MULTIPLE BEARDS)

HUNTER STATE	SUB-SPECIES	BEARDS	LENGTH	SCORE	DATE
1. John Fryatt WI	Eastern	8	70.8750	194.00	4-19-89
2. Chick Shaddox MO	Eastern	7	66.8800	183.75	5-1-86
3. Wm D. Foley AL	Eastern	8	62.500	174.50	4-6-87

GOULDS SUB-SPECIES

HUNTER	SCORE	DATE	STATE
BEST OVERALL GOULDS GOBBLER			
1. George Breton Maynez, Durango Dge., MX	70.50000	4-1-89	DU
2. Hobart O. Pardue, Springfield, LA	65.5000	4-15-87	MX
3. Jamie Bulger	65.0000	4-23-87	CH
HEAVIEST GOULDS GOBBLER			
1. George Breton Maynew Durango Dge., MX	28.0000	4-1-89	DU MX
2. Hobart O. Pardue, Springfield LA	25.5000	4-15-87	
3. Richard C. Kirby, Orchard Park, NY	24.0625	4-10-86	
LONGEST BEARD ON GOULDS GOBBLER			
1. Susan Stoker, Wayzata, MN	12.3750	4-17-87	SO
2. Hobart Pardue, Springfield LA	11.2500	4-15-87	MX
3. David G. Jansma, Waco, TX	11.1250	3-26-85	SN
LONGEST SPURS ON GOULDS GOBBLER			
1. Jamie Bulger, Brewton, AL	1.2500	4-23-89	CH
2. Claibourne Darden Jr, Atlanta, GA	1.1250	4-29-89	SO
George Breton Maynez	1.1250	4-1-89	DU
3. Lynn D. Boykin, Mobile, AL	1.0000	4-21-87	SO
Jerry Crider Cd. Obregon, Sonora, MX	1.0000	4-20-87	MX

Standard Conversions Used in
NWTF Wild Turkey Records

Weight (onces to pounds)		**Measurements** (fractions of an inch)
1 = .0625	9 = .5625	1/8 = .125
2 = .1250	10 = .6250	2/8 = .250
3 = .1875	11 = .6875	3/8 = .375
4 = .2500	12 = .7500	4/8 = .500
5 = .3125	13 = .8125	5/8 = .625
6 = .3750	14 = .8750	6/8 = .750
7 = .4375	15 = .9375	7/8 = .875
8 = .5000		

The shotgun is the favored gun for wild turkey taking. The wild-life managers in some states offer the shotgun as the only legal way to take a spring or fall turkey within their purview. Other states expand the permissible weapons list to include centerfire rifles and muzzleloaders. These states, usually western states, leave the choice of weapons to the individual hunter. That hunter makes his or her choice after evaluating their personal hunting skills and carefully considering their personal turkey hunting goals.

Many dedicated turkey hunters feel that hunters who take a long range turkey with a high power rifle cheat themselves of much of the challenge and excitement of the turkey hunt. Those hunters prefer to enter the turkey woods to contest a turkey gobbler on his home turf. Those hunters utilize preseason scouting, camouflage, woodsmanship and turkey calling skills to bring a puffed up spring gobbler so close they can see the lust in his eyes. A shotgun loaded with birdshot is aimed at the head and the harvest is completed.

The wild turkey has many enemies and few friends in the wild woods. This situation has produced a bird that is epitomized by paranoia. The turkey woods are filled with turkey eaters such as bobcat, coyote, red and gray fox, by a multitude of flying predators who work both the day shift and the night shift, and by man. Each one of them have a highly developed taste for turkey flesh. To survive, the turkey must quickly react to any actual or perceived threat. The turkey does react and does so with considerable enthusiasm in most instances. The paranoia of the wild turkey has caused many firearms manufacturers to develop and market a line of guns specifically designed for the turkey hunter.

That line of special purpose shotguns, although they differ somewhat in configuration as the brand name varies, certainly are more similar than they are dis-similar. The following paragraphs describes the "perfect" turkey gun as it is visualized by at least one hard hunter.

The perfect turkey gun is a twelve gauge shotgun, one that has been chambered to shoot the three inch magnum shell. It is a single barreled gun and is an auto-loader, or if that is not practical, a pump action. The finish on both wood and metal is non-glare, sometimes oil finished wood with no varnish and Parkerized metal as in the Remington SP's or with wood and metal camo painted as in Ithaca's Model 87 Turkey gun.

The perfect turkey gun is short barrelled to make the gun a bit lighter weight and to make the gun more maneuverable in a tight brush situation. Many modern fire arms experts agree that maximum velocity is generated within the first 18" of barrel length.

More barrel does not add one foot to muzzle velocity but in fact may cause a decrease. The superfluous tube causes a friction on the shot string causing a slowdown.

Short barrelled non-reflective shotguns like this Model 87 Ithaca helps the hunter hide.

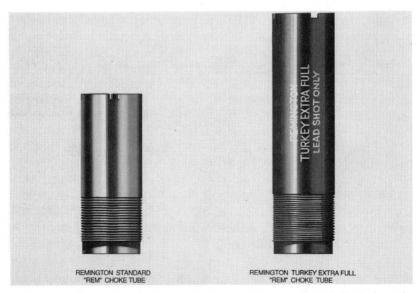

Remington and other manufacturers offer an extra full choke tube for turkey takers, to be used only with lead shot.

The perfect turkey gun will be a fixed full choke, a fixed extra full choke, or come equipped with screw in choke tubes that include full and extra full constrictions. Most of a turkey's big body is well protected by feathers, meat and muscle. Experienced turkey hunters do not shoot at a turkey body. To do so will likely result in a crippling loss. Experienced turkey hunters aim and shoot at a turkey's head and neck, a very vulnerable area. The target, in the case of the head, is about tennis ball sized. The range, in most instances, will vary between 20 yards and forty yards. The turkey gun, obviously, must provide sufficient choke to keep the shot string concentrated.

Finally, the perfect turkey gun will come equipped with sling swivel studs, quick detach swivels, and hopefully a sling so that the gun can be carried comfortably as the hunter makes his or her way through the pre dawn woods or as they make a fast move to close the gap between them and a distant gobble.

There are a number of other guns that will do a fine job for the turkey hunter. Those who prefer a bit more muscle to their turkey taker can choose between one of several of the newly introduced twelve gauges chambered for the 3 1/2" shell. Or they might opt for one of the mightiest mags, a ten gauged gun shooting a 3 1/2" shell. Some hunters might be more comfortable with a bolt action gun such as Marlin's venerable Goose Gun. The following pages will contain a brief description of the author's recommendations, selected in most instances by field evaluation.

The Remington Arms Company now markets the ten gauge auto loader formerly marketed by Ithaca. This biggest of the bangers is the only autoloading ten gauge on the market. It is a junkyard dog kind of gun that has the muscle needed to reach out and touch a turkey causing him to become graveyard dead in an instant. This three shot banger can be bought with a 26" or a 30" barrel. The 26" model makes more sense for the turkey hunter. Those who use the gun to take high flying Canadas, or passage ducks as well as turkeys, might be better satisfied with the longer barrel.

The SP-10 is a handful, weighing a hefty eleven pounds unloaded for the long barrel and a few ounces less for the twenty six inch. Both barrels accept the Rem-Choke screw-in tubes. An extra full tube for turkey hunters is included but can only be used with lead shot.

As is the case with all of the Remington SP (Special Purpose) family, the SP-10 is a gun that will not give the hunter away in the woods. Matte finished metal blends with oil finished wood to make the total gun non-reflective. The big mugger, according to Remington, puts a third more shot into the pattern at 40 yards than do most three inch twelves. The stainless steel gas operated system,

tem, where the cylinder moves rather than the piston, spreads and softens recoil.

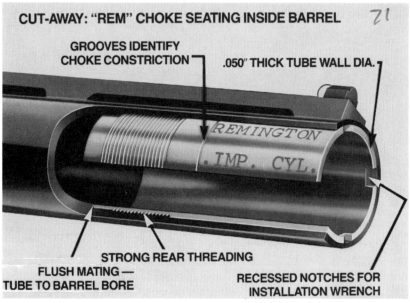

CUT-AWAY: "REM" CHOKE SEATING INSIDE BARREL

GROOVES IDENTIFY
CHOKE CONSTRICTION

.050" THICK TUBE WALL DIA.

REMINGTON .IMP. CYL.

STRONG REAR THREADING

FLUSH MATING —
TUBE TO BARREL BORE

RECESSED NOTCHES FOR
INSTALLATION WRENCH

Cutaway shows design of "Rem" Choke tubes.

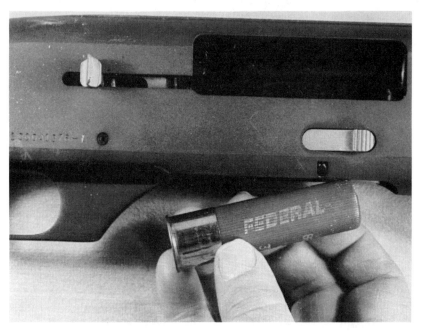

The biggest banger, Remington's SP-10 (formerly the Ithaca Mag-10) accepts a fat 3 1/2" shell.

Browning offers a pump gun chambered for the 3 1/2" ten gauge. This BPS pump can be bought with a barrel length to suit about any taste, anywhere from 24" to 30". The Stalker model of the BPS ten should prove to be popular with turkey hunters. This gun comes equipped with a rugged composite stock that is non-reflective. Metal surfaces are matte finished. Like other guns in the BPS line the BPS-10 comes equipped with Browning's Invector Choke System. Unloaded weight is 9 pounds four ounces for the 24" barrel. Lefties will like the bottom ejection and a convenient tang safety.

Both Browning and Mossberg market a super twelve chambered to accept the 3 1/2" shell. Browning's gun is of the BPS line and is a near clone to the BPS-10. The only discernable difference, other than the chambering, is in weight. The twelve is about a pound lighter.

Mossberg calls their 3 1/2" twelve the Model 835 Ulti-Mag. This heavy duty pump weighs in at seven pounds plus. The gun, in all probability, was engineered on a three inch twelve frame bored out to accept the slightly longer shell. Vent rib and Accu-Mag choke tubes are standard equipment. The stock can be walnut stained hardwood or made of a camo-synthetic. The barrel is back bored to reduce recoil and improve patterns. A tang (thumb) safety offers convenience to right or left handed shooters.

The turkey hunter can find a plentitude of "conventional" three inch twelves marketed with the hide-out hunter in mind. Most U.S. based manufacturers offer guns that are specially engineered to suit those specialized needs.

Author took this fine Merriams using Browning's BPS Stalker in 3" twelve.

Browning offers a three inch twelve in the familiar BPS line. The Stalker comes equipped with a 26" barrel and weighs about seven and a half pounds. This gun accepts the Invector screw-in chokes. Vent rib and recoil pad are standard equipment. As is the case with other 3" guns, 2 3/4" shells can be used as well.

Ithaca's Model 87 is essentially the same pump Ithaca has been marketing these many years. This very successful design has changed little since the days the gun was known as the Ithaca Featherlite. The Model 87 is a five shot that can be bought with a 24" barrel. Vent rib and recoil pad are standard. The gun is available with matte finished metal and oil finished wood or with both metal and wood camo painted. Bottom loading and bottom ejection makes the gun a switch hitter. The gun can be bought with a fixed full choke barrel or with a barrel that accepts screw-in chokes.

Mossberg markets a pump gun chambered for the three inch twelve that has wood and metal covered with special camouflage finish. The receiver is drilled and tapped for scope mounting, a sensible modification for shotguns choked to shoot ultra-tight patterns at up to 40 yards. Vented rib, sling studs, QD swivels and camo sling are standard. The 18 1/2" barrel on the Model 500 Camo Pump causes the gun to weigh in at about seven pounds.

Remington's line of turkey guns has changed little in recent years. This venerable company continues to offer both the 870 SP (a pump) and the Model 11-87 (an autoloader). Both guns come with oil finished wood and matte finished metal. Equipped with a 26" vent rib barrel the Model 870 SP weighs about seven pounds. Recoil pad, sling swivels and camo sling come with the gun.

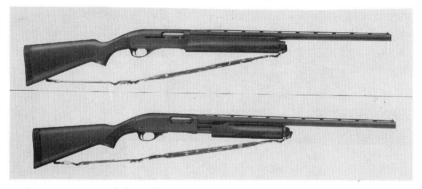

Remington Model 1100 SP (now the 11-87 SP) and the Model 870 SP offer options for hunters who like auto-loaders (top) and pump actions.

The Remington 11-87 SP autoloader weighs a bit more than eight pounds and accepts either 3" or 2 3/4" twelve gauge shells. The screw-in choke system will accept Remington's "Turkey Extra

Full" choke that offers up the extra tight patterns preferred by many turkey hunters.

U.S. Repeating Arms (Winchester) offers a handsome specially engineered turkey gun. The Model 1300 comes equipped with a 22" vent rib barrel that accepts modified, full and extra full choke tubes. Matte finish on the metal makes the gun non-reflective. Camo paint does the same for the stock and the forearm. Turkey hunters who hanker to do their bit for the wild turkey might opt for the National Wild Turkey Federation edition. This gun comes decorated with a strutting gobbler and the initials N.W.T.F. engraved on the left side of the receiver.

U.S. Repeating Arms (Winchester) offers several camo finished models adaptable to turkey hunting.

Some turkey hunters eschew the shotgun in favor of the rifle when it comes time to take turkeys. More than a few force the trusty ought six, their deer and elk gun, to do double duty as a turkey taker. That can be a messy mistake. A big tom turkey in the prime of his gobblerhood might weigh in at 20 plus pounds. Doing the dirty deed to a twenty pound turkey with a gun bored to take a 200 pound mule deer or a 1000 pound elk presents obvious problems. About all such a shooter can do, much of the time, is to make an effort to retrieve the big pieces, collect a few feathers, and go home to cook a nourishing meal that is generous enough to feed a family of one.

The rifle used to take a turkey, obviously, need not be one of the big bores. The group of guns that shoot a .224 diameter bullet can do a decent job if loaded properly and if shot placement is precise. Those guns, listed in ascending case capacity order, are the 22 Hornet, the 218 Bee, the .222 Remington, the .223 Remington, the 222 Remington Magnum, the 219 Donaldson Wasp, the 219 Zipper, the 225 Winchester, the 224 Weatherby Magnum, the 22-250 Remington and its close ballistic clone the 220 Swift. Many of those calibers are designed to shoot the petite .224 pill at speeds that produce spectacular blowup on critters such as prairie dogs, marmots and ground hogs. Those loads will provide an equally spectacular blow up on turkey. It is best to concoct a load that travels at a slower speed, perhaps even down to the slowest accurate velocity.

Slowing the bullet can decrease impact damage but can also decrease the flat shooting potential of the rifle. Range, much of the time, is considerably reduced.

The caliber some shooters call the mighty mouse, the small bored .17, can be a decent to good turkey gun. With proper loading and shot placement the petite 25 grain pill spit out of the .17 Remington can cause a turkey to get dead in a hurry. And can do so without throwing turkey burger and feathers into surrounding zip codes.

A good many western hunters take their turkey with a .22 Winchester Rimfire Magnum. There is little doubt that this gun will kill a turkey if shot placement is precise. The 22 WRFM, however, is basically a short range gun accurate and deadly out to about a hundred yards. Head shots, or a backshot that breaks the backbone, can put a turkey down where he stands. A less perfect shot can cause the big bird to run off, fatally wounded, to die a slow and lingering death. Such a situation is sad for the turkey, sad for the hunter, and sad for the sport.

Which gun is best for a hard hunting turkey taker? They all are. If your bank account allows a specific gun for each type of hunting one of the big bangers, a 3 1/2" ten or a 3 1/2 twelve, might be just the ticket. If your turkey hunting gun must do duty as a goose gun, a duck taker, a cottontail taker, or as a quail gun, you might do better to invest in one of the 3" twelves equipped with choke tubes that permit shooting versatility. If there is a really cold wind blowing through your billfold, and your gun must take critters from coyote size to quail size, take a look at a low cost gun such as the Marlin bolt action twelve, the one they call the Goose Gun.

The gun chosen, properly used and properly cared for, will provide many years of dependable service. And that translates to many happy hunts afield.

TURKEY LOADS AND RELOADS
CHAPTER FIVE

The kind of shell shot from the turkey gun can profoundly affect accuracy and pattern. Experienced turkey hunters have learned the value of patterning shotguns with a variety of shotshell brands, shot/powder combinations, and shot size to learn the type of shotshell their particular gun shoots best.

The crude bead sight of the shotgun does not offer the utmost in accuracy. In many types of shotgun hunting, those where the target flies or runs rapidly, a precise match between the bead and the exact center of the pattern is not crucial. The shooter seldom "aims" the gun at such a target, but instead, shoots instinctively. A moderate discrepancy between point of aim and point of impact seldom affects the outcome. Such is not the case with the turkey hunter. Turkeys are called close. The shot, much of the time, is taken at a stationary or a slowly moving target. That target, the turkey head and neck, is small. A misalignment between bead and impact can cause a miss or cause a crippling loss. A sighting session at the range can verify the agreement between the point the hunter hopes to hit and the point the center of the shot pattern actually strikes.

Hunters who discover a significant misalignment have a couple of options. They can hold "Kentucky windage" to compensate for the misalignment. For those not familiar with the term here is how it is done. If the center of the shot pattern hits five inches to the left of point of aim the shooter simply aims five inches to the right to compensate. The degree of offset needed, unfortunately, does not stay constant at all ranges and this makes this response unacceptable to the turkey hunter who is serious about the sport. The second option, more costly and more time consuming, involves taking the gun to a gunsmith to have the barrel bead relocated to more closely match the pattern.

Some dedicated hunters have abandoned the barrel bead entirely in favor of a more sophisticated sighting system. Those hunters reason that tightly choked turkey guns shoot nearly like a rifle at ranges closer than 20 or 25 yards and must be aimed just as a rifle is aimed. Some have their turkey gun tapped and drilled to accept telescope sight mounts and then install a low power telescope sight. Others wishing a more sophisticated sighting system do as those who shotgun for deer do, they choose a gun equipped with both rear and front sights, or they choose another sight option such as the Aimpoint.

A visit to the range to punch paper can be helpful to shotshooters in another way. Nearly every shotgun shoots a particular size shot, perhaps even a particular brand a bit the best. A session at the range can let the shooter discover the kind of fodder his or her gun prefers. Here is the way experienced hunters pattern their guns.

Nearly every shotgun shoots one shot size or brand better.

Obtain a quantity of paper large enough to hold a circle with a 30" diameter. Some art supply stores offer tablets large enough so that individual sheets can be used. Butcher paper will also do decently. Newspaper sheets, although of the right size and available, work less well because the print makes it more difficult to discover and count the penetrations.

Use a broad tipped marking pencil to draw the 30" circle on each of the sheets. At the exact center of the circle draw on an approximation of a turkey gobbler's head and neck. If you distrust your artistic abilities, a facsimile of a turkey head and neck, with vital areas bold lined, can be ordered from Real Turkeys, 2201 S.E. 41st Avenue, Gainesville, Florida 32601.

Measure off forty yards at the range and place the paper target on a sturdy support such as a target frame or a cardboard box. Move back to the 40 yard line and use a bench rest to AIM at a point midway between the point where the neck hits the shoulder and the head. Fire five rounds of each ammunition tested and record the results in a notebook. Noting the position of the densest part of the pattern and comparing that to the point of aim can reveal if the barrel bead is positioned correctly. Counting the holes within the 30 inch circle and comparing that to the number of shot packed into the load will reveal choke efficiency. Consult the chart provided to learn the number of shot in many of the most used loads. If the load you use is not listed, check with your firearms dealer. Most have charts that show shot capacity. This will reveal choke efficiency.

A measure of the pattern density, a most important aspect, can be learned by inspecting the number of pellets that cluster around the fatal area of the head and neck. Finally, as a more specific measure, count the number of pellets that actually penetrate the vital areas. What is good and what is bad when it comes to pattern density? Many of the tightly choked turkey guns on the market will deliver patterns that approach ninety percent. Put another way, nine of ten available pellets falls within the 30" circle.

There is no consensus among turkey hunters on the shot size best suited for turkey hunting. Every experienced hunter has his or her own idea on shot size. If every hunter called every bird to less than forty yards, and if every gun patterned exactly as aimed, shot size would not be important. All birdshot sizes, in all likelihood, would be capable of penetrating a turkey's head or neck to make a clean kill. As this "ideal" shot is seldom offered, turkey hunters should consider a number of facts before they decide on the correct size shot for their turkey hunting.

Foremost, the bones of a turkey's head are thin and offer little resistance to penetration. Velocity at normal ranges is not a problem. Small shot sizes offer an obvious advantage. More of the shot can be packed into the case and that translates to denser patterns. Denser patterns increase the likelihood of a hit. And even one pellet in a vital area will kill a turkey as dead as need be.

Using buckshot during spring turkey season is prohibited in many states and can pose a danger to other hunters.

Shooting small shot sizes in turkey guns can cause the sport of turkey hunting to become more safe. Accidental shootings can and do occur. Not often, to be sure, but one time is one too many. A hunter shot with a shot shell loaded with a small size shot has an increased chance of recovery. The heavier the shot size the more the likelihood of a fatal or crippling wound.

How small is too small? Long time turkey hunter Lovett Williams recommends #6 shot but sees nothing wrong with moving to 7 1/2's if they happen to pattern best in your particular gun.

A good many hunters advocate shooting a small shot size as the first shot and chambering in a larger shot size as a backup "killer". There is a fallacy in that line of reasoning. If the small shot size is the best option for a standing or slowly moving turkey, why wouldn't that same round be the best choice for a turkey who is getting gone as fast as his legs or wings will carry him? Shooting a round loaded with large diameter shot at a turkey that has been crippled with small shot can doom that crippled turkey to a slow death. Turkeys will survive a hit with small diameter shot in many instances. Those same turkeys seldom survive a hit with the larger shot.

Hunters who happen to own a turkey gun that is poorly choked, one that does not deliver at least eighty percent pattern to a 30" circle at 40 yards, can avoid the cost of a new gun by having their current gun modified. Competent gunsmiths can install a screw in choke system or can install a forcing cone into the barrel bore to dramatically increase pattern density. Mark Bansner, a Pennsylvania gunsmith, specializes in such modifications. He can be contacted by writing Bansner's Gunsmithing Specialties, 261 East Main Street, Adamstown, PA 19501.

Factory loaded rifle rounds can be destructive. Reloading is recommended.

Turkey hunters who rifle hunt for turkeys, and who have the equipment and knowledge needed to reload, have an advantage over hunters who do not reload. Factory loaded ammunition is loaded too hot for the turkey hunter. The bird will be killed, sure enough, but will likely be killed a lot deader than need be. Hand-loaders can reduce the velocity of the bullet to do away with much of the explosive tissue destruction.

These hot loaded 22-250's, accurate and effective on varmints, would likely send a Missouri turkey to visit Chicago.

All reloaders should own at least one current data reloading manual. The Hornaday Handbook of Cartridge Reloading (Third Edition) is a good one. So is Sierra Bullets Second Edition Reloading Manual. Each of the books mentioned include charts that show minimum and maximum velocity loads for each caliber. The lowest velocity load for the .222 Remington, as an example, is listed at 2700 fps muzzle velocity when shooting a 55 grain bullet. A hand loading turkey hunter who wished to develop a rifle load that would kill a turkey and leave a bit of dignity to the carcass should start with that low velocity load and test fire for accuracy. By increasing the load in half grain increments, and test firing each loading, the hunter could develop a load that was both accurate and effective.

Rifle shooters should avoid shots at the meaty part of the turkey breast. The breast of the wild turkey, more so than in the domestic strains, is the main part of the meal. Damage there puts a bullet hole through the best part of the Thanksgiving dinner. It is better to aim at the place where the wing butt joins the body if the bird presents a side view. If the turkey is facing away, a hit high up on the backbone will anchor the turkey in his tracks and destroy very little of the tasty flesh.

Shot Size	Ounces and pellets in load								
	1	1⅛	1¼	1⅜	1½	1⅝	1¾	1⅞	2
7½	355	394	438	481	525	569	613	657	701
6	255	253	281	309	338	366	394	422	431
5	170	191	212	234	255	276	297	318	339
4	135	152	169	186	203	219	236	253	270
2	90	102	113	124	135	146	157	168	180
BB	50	56	63	69	75	81	87	93	100

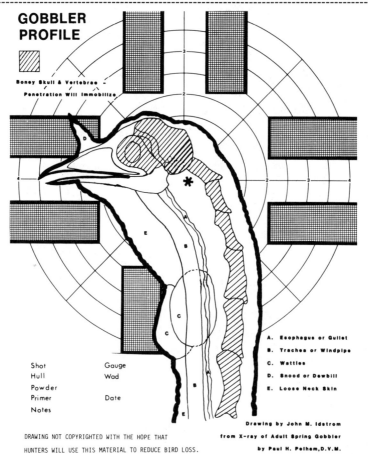

GOBBLER PROFILE

Boney Skull & Vertebrae -
Penetration Will Immobilize

A. Esophagus or Gullet
B. Trachea or Windpipe
C. Wattles
D. Snood or Dewbill
E. Loose Neck Skin

Shot   Gauge
Hull   Wad
Powder
Primer   Date
Notes

Drawing by John M. Idstrom

from X-ray of Adult Spring Gobbler
by Paul H. Pelham,D.V.M.

DRAWING NOT COPYRIGHTED WITH THE HOPE THAT
HUNTERS WILL USE THIS MATERIAL TO REDUCE BIRD LOSS.

This chart can be Xerox enlarged to 8 1/2" x 11" and used as a patterning target.

48

MAKING A GOOD GUN BETTER
CHAPTER SIX

The gang of turkey guns on the market can be good news to the hunter whose wallet is crammed with tens and twenties, money not dedicated to certain luxuries of life such as food, clothing and enough Pampers to keep the kid's bottoms at least semi-dry. Most of us, maybe even all, fall into that sad economic bracket at some point in our lives. To those hunters, the purchase of one of the new special purpose guns specifically designed for the hide out hunter is a pleasant fantasy. Those MB (mighty broke) hunters have another option or two that will allow them to own a good gun without forcing the kids to eat grits during the summer months.

The first option is obvious. Buy a used gun rather than a new gun. Visiting the local gun dealers might be a good first step. Look over the used guns on display. Chances are good that one of those experienced guns will exactly fit both your needs and your budget. If not, watch the want ads during the off season. It may even pay to run an advertisement of your own listing what you want and what you have to pay. Offer to trade if you have an item of similar value that is not needed. Offer to work if you have a skill that can be converted to trade.

The reflective finish on this gun nearly caused this Arizona hunter to lose his chance at a trophy.

If you do not find the gun you want at a price you can afford to pay locally, go national. Gun List, an indexed publication, contains thousands of advertisements from folks who have new and used guns they hope to sell. Much of the time the selling price is considerably below the current retail price. For a subscription write to Gun List, 700 East State Street, Iola WI 54990.

There is a good chance that you already own a shotgun that can be turned into a hide out turkey gun with a bit of effort and a bit of money.

Competent gunsmiths like Mark Bansner (mentioned in Chapter 3) can do a job on a good gun that makes it better. The process involves shortening the barrel to turkey hunter length, maybe 20 inches, and then installing a forcing cone that chokes the gun to the tight patterns turkey hunters need. The cost? Not cheap but considerably less than the cost of a new gun.

Western hunter Larry Gates took this fine New Mexico Merriams using a Bansner modified ten gauge.

A second option is having the barrel shortened and then fitted to accept one of the efficient screw-in choke systems on the market. A hunter who uses the gun for a variety of game could change chokes as needed to best meet the demands of that particular hunt.

Hunters who hesitate to radically modify the barrel on Ol' Betsey can consider the purchase of a new barrel. Hastings (P.O. Box 224, Clay Center, Kansas 67432) offers replacement barrels for many of the popular models of shotguns. Hunters have a choice of barrel length and choke. Many of the replacement barrels come equipped with a choke system that makes the gun a versatile multi-species performer.

Compare the finish on the two guns and guess which one of these happy hunters tied their tag to a turkey's leg.

If your present gun is acceptable as is except for minor deficiencies, a fine tuning may be all that is needed to turn the gun into a solid turkey gun. Here are minor modifications that can make your good gun better.

Many factory produced guns leave the dealer with blued and highly polished metal and varnished wood. Mighty pretty. The trouble is, those polished surfaces are highly reflective and can cause a paranoid tom turkey to take off like Man of War leaving the gate. A serious turkey hunter must do something to reduce the shine, or accept the sad fact that many (maybe even most) of his or her trips afield will turn into "nature appreciation" outings. Here are ways to uglify your gun so that it will be invisible to the turkey and beautiful to the turkey hunter.

Medium fine steel wool rubbed with the grain of the wood will do much to satinize the glossy finish. Camo tape applied to wood and metal does a decent job of disguising the glare. The tape can be purchased in a variety of color and pattern to somewhat match the kind of woods you hunt.

Some hunters opt for a more permanent uglification. They use a flat metal paint to camo paint the wood and the metal of their main turkey taker. Although this treatment is somewhat permanent, the paint can be removed from the metal with a bit of effort. The author once purchased a used Sako Forester in 22-250 caliber to use as a coyote whacker. The previous owner had camo taped the handsome wood stock and had brushed a heavy coat of metal paint onto the bull barrel. Elbow grease and strong language removed the tape. The painted metal was more of a challenge, but was eventually removed using a paint remover developed for use on the painted aluminum found on aircraft. The deep Sako blue below was not affected.

Bell & Carlson offer a camouflaged replacement stock for many rifles and shotguns.

Hunters who have a hankering to go first class can purchase one of the finely crafted replacement stocks now on the market. The author has composite camo painted replacement stocks marketed by Bell & Carlson (604 N. 4th Street, Atwood KS 67730) on many of his guns, both rifles and shotguns. The replacement stocks are of moderate cost and do a fine job of turning a beater into a beauty. Installation is simply a matter of removing two or three bolts, removing the old stock, positioning the new stock, and rebolting. The rifle replacement stocks are free-floated so that a minimum amount of fine fitting is needed.

Every turkey hunter will be convinced, after a few trips to the woods, that a carrying sling is a convenience he or she should not do without. If your gun is fitted with sling swivel studs and QD swivels it is a simple matter of purchasing a carrying strap and attaching the ends to the swivels. Most of the mail order catalogue companies offer carrying straps, some in camo. Check Cabela's (812 13th Avenue, Sidney, NE 69160), Bass Pro Shops (1935 S. Campbell, Springfield, MO 65898-4046), or Gander Mountain (Box 248, Hwy W., Wilmot, WI 53192). Prices range from a modest five bucks up to about ten times that.

If your gun is not equipped with sling swivel studs it is a simple matter to install them. Check the catalog companies mentioned above for both the studs and for QD (quick detach) swivels. Another source is Michael's of Oregon (P.O. Box 13010, Portland, OR 97213). Michael's sells their products through retail outlets like sporting goods stores and discount merchandisers such as K-Mart and Wal-Mart. Writing the company can produce information directing you to the nearest dealer.

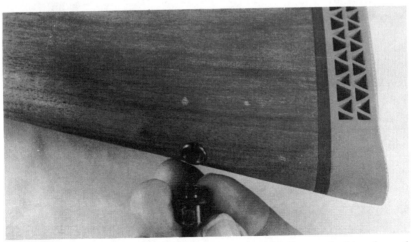

Many modern shotguns come equipped with sling swivel studs and recoil pads. Those that do not can be modified with little effort.

Attaching sling swivel studs to a gun is a job that requires a few minutes of time and a few tools. Do not attempt to screw the studs into the stock without first drilling access holes. To do so will almost surely result in a split stock. Mark the position on the stock the swivel studs are to be placed and stick on a piece of masking tape to protect the stock. Use a punch to lightly indent the wood as a starting point for the drill. Use a drill bit a size smaller than the diameter of the screw stud to drill a hole that is as deep as the screws on the stud. Use a small wrench to screw the stud into the pilot hole.

Many models of shotguns require a screw in stud only for the stock stud. The front stud, much of the time, is fitted directly onto the hardware of the forearm keeper and no drilling is necessary.

Many of the guns used for turkey hunting are lightweight and that is an advantage. Many also are chambered to accept either a 3" or 3 1/2" inch maximum loaded shell, another plus. Those two aspects, however, can cause the hunter to seriously consider the installation of a recoil pad if the gun is not already so equipped.

Adding a recoil pad to the stock of a shotgun adds about an inch to overall length. As many shotgun stocks are made to fit the "average" man or woman, adding an inch to the length is desireable. If the stock perfectly fits as it is, it will be necessary to saw off a bit of the stock. If the stock is much too long, now might be the time to consider the length that will be added by the pad and shorten the stock so that it is right fitting.

The actual installation of the recoil pad can go quickly. Choose a pad that is larger than the one you need so that it may be filed down to maintain the curve of the stock. Remove the butt plate from the stock and hold the pad in place. Much of the time the screw holes that held the butt plate can be used to attach the recoil pad. Use the long screws provided to screw through the back of the recoil pad into the wood of the stock. The heads of the screws will sink through the cushion of the pad to snug against the hard plastic plate next to the butt of the stock.

A final modification that can make a good gun better is the installation of a sighting aid. It has been mentioned that the short barrel of the turkey gun does not reduce velocity but may in fact increase velocity. There is a small price to be paid, however, if the barrel is significantly shortened. The "sighting plane" of the barrel is reduced. The greater distance between the barrel bead and the eye in long barreled guns can increase sighting efficiency. That advantage leaves when the barrel is shortened. As a compensation a second barrel bead can be installed to the rear of the front bead. The lining up of the two beads helps the shooter to stay on target.

Some hunters go a step farther and have their gun tapped to accommodate telescope sight mounts. A low power telescope sight such as the Bushnell 1.5x4.5 variable can cause the tight choked turkey gun to shoot like a rifle. Other devices, like the Aimpoint (203 Elden Street, Herndon, VA 22070) sight can significantly increase shotshell accuracy.

Many turkeys have made their way to that big feedlot in the sky because a good hunter used a non-specialized gun efficiently. Turkeys can be called and killed using out of the box factory guns that shine like polished marble. A good many have also escaped with their lives because something about the set up gave the turkey a small excuse to become terrified. Customizing the turkey gun sure can't hurt and will likely help. That alone is reason enough for modification.

A shiny gun can cause a paranoid tom turkey to get gone enthusiastically. (Photo Mich. Dept of Nat. Resources).

CAMOUFLAGE
CHAPTER SEVEN

Turkey hunters who are long of tooth can recall going afield to hunt turkey in the same set of clothes they wore to work (some still do). And those hunters killed turkeys. Shortly after World War II, when surplus military camo clothing became available, some hunters decided "if it works for the marines it might work for me" and bought a good deal of the leaf green surplus camo pants and jackets, to cause the fall woods to look a bit military. Not many years later camo hunting clothing became available in a great diversity of color and pattern. Some hunters, actually a good many, would rather go to the turkey woods stark naked than go without the proper pattern of camouflage pants, shirts, jackets, gloves, shoes, cap, facemask, and most likely, skivvies. A good many of those hunters (if they have money left to buy shells) also take turkey. Considering all of that, does a turkey hunter really need all of that camouflage material to call a turkey close? Many experienced turkey hunters would answer in the negative. One high profile turkey hunter, chairing a seminar to teach tactics and techniques, summed it up succinctly. "I would rather go to the woods with a hunter who wears red overalls and sits still," he said, "than hunt with a fully camouflaged person who is a squirmer."

Face paint hides the face but can be messy and offers little protection from blood (and grease) loving insects.

Remaining as motionless as humanly possible can be critical to success when the hunter is working a paranoid tom. That means no swatting at gnats or mosquitos, no scratching, and no friendly waves to your hunting partner. Even though a turkey has color vision, sitting motionless is almost surely more important than what the hunter wears. The wearing of clothing that blends inconspicuously into the background runs a close second in importance.

Like men, turkey are not all created equal, particularly when it comes to a consideration of paranoia. Some turkeys, the teenagers many turkey hunters call jakes, can be pathetically naive. Some fully mature turkeys, longbeards who should know better, can also be trusting if they have not led the hard life of a hard hunted turkey. At the other end of the paranoia spectrum is the turkey who has come to a hunter's call a time or two and who has heard the thunder of a Mag twelve, perhaps even felt the sting of one or two fast travelling number six shot. That turkey loses all of his trust in lovesick hen yelps in an instant. The next time that turkey responds to a spring invitation he will do so reluctantly and will be enthusiastically alert. The slightest suspicion will cause that turkey to eschew all thoughts of love and turn his entire attention to the important task of getting the hell gone.

Remington's Ultimate Climate Suit (shown here in Mossy Oak pattern) is waterproof and is made with many gear pockets. (Remington Photo).

Turkey hunters who wear camouflage clothing to the turkey woods, and that takes in just about all of them, can pick and choose from colors and patterns that closely match the conditions current in their neck of the woods. Trebark, the popular pattern developed by Jim Crumley ten years ago, provides a close match to the hardwood bark pattern found through much of the best eastern wild turkey range. Bill Jordan's Realtree does the same. Mossy Oak carries a pattern that blends best with the big white oaks of the South. There is a camo pattern for hunters who hunt the pines and even patterns for hunters who spend a good part of their time hunting snow turkeys. This diversity of pattern, upon sober reflection, makes a lot of sense. The purpose of any camouflage is to disguise the wearer and make him or her blend into the background. Common sense tells us that a hunter completely outfitted in one of the tree bark patterns would certainly not be inconspicuous if he was to set up in the middle of a snowbank. Under those circumstances, a set of painters coveralls would be preferable.

Camo clothing comes in a variety of weights and fabrics also. Some sets are insulated for cold weather hunts. Others are made of mesh to permit comfortable hunting in climates where the sun seldom sets.

At least one businessman offers custom made camo. Ben James, doing business as B.J.'s Custom Clothing (209 Water Street, Washington, GA 30673) keeps right busy tailoring camouflage. Customers pick the pattern, pick the weight of the cloth, decide if they wish single weight garments or those that are insulated and lined, and then supply the necessary measurements. Ben does the rest and does so at a price that is competitive.

Complete camo is recommended for turkey hunting. That means pants and shirt, or jacket, of course, but means also that the hunter who hopes to be completely safe should wear camouflage gloves and a head net. Both the head net and the gloves can do double duty. They hide the flash of a hunters hand or his face. And they offer protection from the hordes of hungry blood suckers that hunt the hunters who hunt the turkeys. Mosquitos, gnats, ticks and others of like persuasion.

Hunting boots made partly of a camo design nylon or Goretex are also available. The boots are almost all light in weight and some have the added asset of being water resistant. Make it a particular point to examine the boot soles. On the set-up the boot bottoms will be the most visible part of the boot from a turkey's viewpoint. Avoid soles that are made of white or cream colored material. Here are other tips that might help in the selection of proper camouflage.

Buy a head net made of netting that pulls completely over the head and extends down past the neck onto the shoulder. Pick a head net without eyeholes. Such a head net will offer the best camouflage and will serve as a netting to protect your face and neck from the blood suckers. Pick gloves thick enough to keep your hands from freezing but light enough so that you can get your gloved finger into the trigger guard of the gun. Take a close look at gloves or mittens that are constructed with a slit that lets the trigger finger escape when the moment of truth comes.

Face and shoulder netting provides concealment and protection from mosquitos, gnats and flies.

Wear a camo cap rather than a camo hat with a floppy brim. Bush hats look good in advertisements and when worn by macho actors on the screen. They are a bother in the turkey woods as it seems every other limb takes a whack at them and you spend a good deal of your hunting time hunting down your hat. Caps stay on the head better and have an added advantage. Caps have a bill that can be used to shade out a low sun.

Eyeholes in head net improve visibility but offer insect access. (Hunter's Specialties Photo).

Sun glare off of this hunter's wrist watch (arrow) can alarm a paranoid turkey.

Choose layered camo rather than a single set of heavy- weights. Turkey hunters spend a good deal of time setting shivering in the pre-dawn darkness waiting for a roosted gobbler to fly down. They need to keep warm. After the sun comes up however, maybe about mid morning, some spring days turn downright warm. It is an advantage to be able to peel off the clothing as the temperature warms.

Avoid camo clothing that is single stitched. Some such, usually outfits made overseas of the cheapest material available, will rip the first time the hunter comes within one hundred yards of a barbed wire fence.

Also avoid camo material that is stiff to the touch and shiny to the eye. Much of the time this type of camo will scream and shout each time it is scraped by a limb. Look for material that is soft and non-reflective.

Purchase a camo fanny pack or day pack to take along on scouting forays or on hunts. Turkey hunters often carry a lot of gear. Calls, extra shells, a compact camera, water, a compass, topo maps, knife and maybe even a granola bar or two. Those items are easier carried, and more accessible, when they are organized into a day pack or a fanny pack. Choose a pack that is made of non reflective material if possible.

Include an extra pair of gloves and a spare head net in the fanny pack as backups. Those two items are often lost. Working without either can make an already difficult task much more difficult.

Include a few black plastic garbage bags (30 gallon size) in the pack. In the event of a sudden rain you can tear a head hole and a pair of armholes to construct a makeshift raincoat. If you come to a creek you must cross, and are the kind of hunter who worries about wet feet, place a leg into a sack and tie the top of the sack up above the knee. This emergency wader should get you across a shallow creek with dry feet. These emergency waders can slip on rocks. Use caution.

Include a few Ziplock plastic bags (1 gallon size) in the pack. One can be used to hold the heart, liver and gizzard of your turkey. Another can be used to protect the compact camera you carry to record the magic moment. Still another can be used to hold and protect any loose feathers that fall from the turkey as he flops about. If the bird is to be mounted, the taxidermist will be able to replace those feathers.

If you use a box call or a slate, carry an empty bread wrapper in your pack. A box call does not work well if the wood is wet. If it starts to rain as you work your turkey, place your call and your hands inside the bread wrapper. The box will be kept dry and the quality of the sound will not be materially affected.

Do the same with a slate call if your peg is of wood. If the peg is of Plexiglass you will be able to produce decent yelps clucks and purrs even if slate and peg are wet.

Be aware that the purpose of camouflage is to keep the turkey unaware of your presence. A turkey has a poorly developed sense of smell so there is small worry on that count. A turkey does have excellent eyesight however, and better than average hearing. Be aware that noise camo is just as important as sight camouflage. Do not talk with a companion as you walk the turkey woods. You could hear a gobble at about any time. Conversation that the turkey can overhear can ruin a potential opportunity to work a longbeard.

Do not go afield with material in your pockets that clang or jangle together. Leave loose change at home or in the ashtray of your car. Examine sling swivels on your gun to be sure there is no possibility of metal to metal contact. Use a stout rubber band to keep the paddle of the box call tight to the lips. A good many turkey have panicked out of the country because the box squeaked discordantly at precisely the wrong time.

Many turkey hunters succeed because they are attentive to small details. The turkey certainly does, and the hunter who does not is giving a worthy opponent an unnecessary advantage.

A properly camouflaged Oklahoma hunter shown an instant before the "moment of truth".

DECOYS
CHAPTER EIGHT

Have you heard the story of the hunter who travelled to Africa to hunt elephant? He had to cut his hunt short. He ruptured himself carrying the decoys. Bad joke? Sure it is. But the joke makes a point. Almost every type of hunting, excepting elephant hunting, can be improved upon if a decoy is properly used. Turkey hunting is no exception.

Using a decoy on a turkey hunt, it should be noted, can sometimes be as deadly to the hunter as it is to the hunted. Spring turkey hunters don full camouflage to hide out in the bushes making a noise like a tom turkey's girlfriend. That alone can be hazardous. Some fellow hunters, too eager or too inexperienced, key in on the turkey sounds to take a "sound shot". Nationwide, a few turkey hunters are accidentally shot by other hunters each year. Adding a decoy to an already potentially hazardous situation can compound the danger. Almost every long time turkey hunter can tell a tale of an overeager hunter shooting up another hunter's decoy. The fact that the target in the spring is a male turkey, a gobbler, and that the decoy is always a hen, an illegal target, does not seem to deter those who gun the decoys. Having said that, it is also proper to say that a properly positioned decoy poses small threat to the hunter and can substantially increase that hunter's chance of tying his tag to the scaly leg of a longbearded gobbler.

This posed picture shows variety of decoys available.

The hen turkey decoy is a part of the standard equipment for archery hunters. Those who hanker to take a turkey using stick and string must have the bird close, much closer than in the case of a gun hunter, must keep the bird in close for a time, and must have something there to divert the bird's attention as they draw and release. The turkey decoy helps in each of those aspects. The turkey decoy can do the same for the shotgun hunter, even though the shot shooter has the advantage of extended range and a more efficient weapon.

Turkey decoys can be particularly helpful in open or semi- open areas. A turkey gobbler can strut or sneak into view to a point where he can see the place from where the enticing calls originate. The gobbler is lovesick and is naive. He is not stupid. That turkey expects to see the hen turkey he has heard. If his eyes do not verify what his ears have heard, he is not likely to come one step closer. That hung up turkey will stay out of shotgun range to display each of his irresistible maneuvers. He will strut. He will gobble. He will strut and gobble at the same time. He may drum and pffft. If all else fails he will squat to a very awkward position and masturbate. He will do all of that but he will not come one step closer.

The use of a turkey decoy can permit the turkey to see what he expects to see. The decoy is a suspicion remover also. If that silly hen is standing right out in the open and is safe, his turkey brain tells him, then it is surely safe for me to strut right on in to give that hen a little bit of what she desperately wants.

Every turkey in the woods does not react to a decoy in the same way. Some gobbler gangs come at a hard run, racing to see which is permitted first crack and which has to take sloppy seconds. Some turkeys will strut right up to the plastic imitation turkey and do his best to mount. When the decoy falls on its side, as it almost always does, some persistent gobblers will do their best to copulate into the wing, an act that is comical to watch, and truthfully, has small chance of success. Other turkeys, apparently equally ardent, will take one quick look at the decoy and turn to make a break for home and mother. Nothing, not even a decoy, works one hundred percent of the time.

Hunters have a number of commercially made decoys to choose from. Some are simple silhouettes. Others are full bodied decoys. Others are simply shells that look full bodied from a distance but are hollow inside. One type of decoy is inflatable. Every one, with the possible exception of the silhouette, can fool some turkeys.

Some hunters have used a few hours of spare time to carve out their own decoy, usually of styrofoam, and have used spray paint to give the styrofoam a somewhat turkey like appearance. Some have added authenticity by attaching the folded wings from an actual turkey. This is a practice that certainly adds to the decoy but is a practice that may increase the risk a turkey hunter faces. Much of the time the wings added have been removed from a tom turkey. The difference in the wing pattern could cause an overeager hunter to mistake the decoy for a male turkey.

Hen fluffs aggressively as gobbler displays for a hen turkey decoy.

Experienced turkey hunters place the decoy no more than fifteen yards away from their set-up. Some gobblers will hang up twenty or so yards out away from the decoy to display. Having the decoy somewhat close puts that hung up gobbler at extreme risk if the hunter is holding a three inch twelve or something larger.

Position the decoy so that no hunter can approach unseen to a place that puts the decoy between you and him (or her). To do so puts you in a risky spot if the hunter decides to blast away.

It is almost certain that the immovability of the turkey decoy can cause the amorous tom to develop doubts. Some hunters add "life" to the decoy by attaching a string to the decoy and running that string to their setup. A gentle tug on the string will cause the plastic turkey to make a small movement.

If one decoy is good are two decoys twice as good? Probably not, although the use of decoys is so new to turkey hunting that there are few absolute answers. Two decoys may be better than one. Three may be better than two. This is a matter that needs serious field testing. Based on his experience hunting several sub-species of the wild turkey, the author uses a gang of decoys when they are available, figuring that too many is better than not enough.

The decoy is best used as a spring hunting aid. The legal bird then is a gobbler and the decoy is a hen, a situation that offers some protection to the hunter. The use of a decoy in the fall, when any turkey is usually a legal target, can increase the danger dramatically. Are decoys effective in the fall? Probably so. A turkey that comes to the call in the fall usually comes because he or she is lonesome for another turkey. Fall turkeys are gregarious. Hens and their broods join with other hens with broods. Jakes sometimes run in teenage gangs. Even the old gobblers move about in bachelor bands. When one of those groups is dispersed, either as a hunter makes a scatter or because of a predator attack, flock members develop an urge to reflock. As is the case with the spring bird, the fall bird expects to see a turkey at the spot where he has heard a turkey. If he does not, particularly if that turkey happens to be a longbeard, he is not likely to stay around for long.

A final word on the use of decoys for the fall hunt. For safety sake, let the decoy rest until spring season rolls around. You do not need a decoy to take a fall turkey. The small advantage offered is not worth the risk.

The main strength of the decoy is likely as a tool for the archer and as a tool for the caller who is armed with a camera. The decoys bring the birds closer than they would otherwise come. The decoy serves as a suspicion remover and tends to keep the turkey around the setup for a longer period of time. Finally, the decoy gives the turkey something to look at, an attention diverter as it were, while the archer or the photographer does the dirty deed.

The lack of visibility in these Wisconsin woods limits the effectiveness of this decoy gang.

COMPETITION CALLING
CHAPTER NINE

A person with limited hearing, or no sense of hearing at all, can have fun at a turkey calling contest. Most contestants put on an enjoyable show as they prance and posture before the audience. Those who participate in the owl hooting competition are particularly active. There are reasons other than showmanship for these antics, according to Preston Pittman, a very successful contest caller and the owner of his own turkey call manufacturing business. The posturing, according to Preston, is not for the benefit of the judges. They are seated out of sight of the contestants to preserve the anonymity of the individual contestant. The posturing is not done mainly for the benefit of the audience, although many of the more experienced competitors are showmen and enjoy playing to the spectators. The posturing, much of the time, helps the contestant with air control. Certain body postures facilitate the critical aspects of air expulsion, so important to contestants who use air activated devices like the diaphragm or the natural voice.

World champion turkey caller Ray Eye is on the Pro-Staff for H.S. Strut and recently authored Hunting Wild Turkeys with Ray Eye and has marketed a video (Eye on the Wild Turkey) dealing with wild turkey hunting.

Many turkey calling contests offer a junior division.

The sometimes humorous posturing, according to Pittman, can help the contestant in one other way. Playing to the crowd gains audience support and that helps the contestant to get psyched up for his performance.

Calling to judges is considerably different from calling to a wild turkey. The main difference is basic. Wild turkeys seldom expect perfection in the turkey talk they hear. The men and women who judge turkey calling contests almost always do. There are other important differences. Basic turkey will seldom impress a turkey contest judge, and a real turkey would score poorly. Most experienced competitors have learned to add flourishes. Preston Pittman, as an example, does his best to put a "southern drawl" into his yelps, cuts and cackles, hoping to sound different from other callers.

Becoming successful on the competition turkey calling circuit has many rewards. Significant cash and merchandise awards go to the winners. Considerable prestige comes with the awards. Consistent winners have the opportunity to become field reps for major turkey call manufacturers and are sometime paid handsomely for the use of their name. Some, a lot in actuality, parlay contest calling success, and the name recognition that is a concomitant, into successful business enterprises. The names Paul Butski, Jim Clay, Kelly Cooper, Ray Eye, Dick Kirby, Preston Pittman and Eddie Salter come immediately to mind. A lot of others.

Contestants call to out of sight judges. (World Champion Paul Butski shown at the 1987 Grand National Calling Championships).

Champion caller Dick Kirby has parlayed his turkey calling skills into a successful business (Quaker Boy Inc.).

The competition success that permits all of those positive results does not come without effort. The route Preston Pittman used to travel from obscurity to the top of the competition calling world is somewhat typical.

Preston's Dad took him to the Mississippi State Turkey Calling Contest when Preston was 13 years old. While there Preston had the opportunity to visit with a turkey caller by the name of Jack Dudley, a man who called using his natural voice.

Dudley became the young Pittman's idol and he used Dudley's turkey call instruction record to practice, using his natural voice just as Jack did. A few years later, when he was 16 years old, Preston returned to the Mississippi State Turkey Calling Contest and used his natural voice to turkey talk his way to the championship.

The main element to contest calling success, in Preston Pittman's opinion, is practice, practice, and more practice. He suggests that neophyte callers attend turkey calling contests in their areas to tape record the presentation of the finalists. Later, back at home, those tapes can be played and replayed, with special attention paid to the performance of the winners. Practice with the call, using the taped sounds as a guide, can cause proficiency. More good advice from Preston Pittman follows.

It is important, he says, to know the individuals who will judge the contest. Each judge has his or her own likes and dislikes. Some, as an example, might award a higher score to callers who put a lot of rasp into their calls. Call raspy to those judges or you may lose points.

What a caller does before he walks out on the stage to compete can influence success or failure. Preston uses that time to psyche himself up for the performance, convincing himself that he is as good or better than any other contestant, building confidence. The pre-contest time can be advantageously used in one other way. Use that opportunity to talk to the master of ceremonies. Be sure you understand the rules of the contest. If the rules stipulate that the contestants are allowed two repetitions of each of the calls, do not produce three repetitions. To do so might cause automatic disqualification, even though the calls are perfect. Overcalling can have another negative effect. Any mistake can cost points. The more a competitor calls the more apt he or she is to make a mistake.

Contestants should do some practice under somewhat the same conditions they will face in the actual contest. If the contest is to be held in a metal building (a setting that can affect tonal perception) then some practice should be done in a metal building. Tape that practice and play that recording back to discover the effect the acoustic setting has on tonal perception.

Preston feels it is important to do pre-contest practice before an audience. A contestant who practices in the privacy of his home, too many times, gets stage fright when he is asked to perform before several hundred spectators. And that crowd of humanity, almost always, will cause the tone of the calls to sound differently than calls made in an empty building.

The best kind of call to use, according to Preston, is that call the contestant feels most competent with. Preston learned to call with his natural voice and has won many championships natural voicing the calls. The human voice, sad to say, is not always a dependable instrument. A cold, a sinus infection, laryngitis or even congestion can put the caller out of action. Preston still uses his natural voice to make some calls but has learned to make those same calls with a diaphragm.

Preston Pittman is a very successful contest caller and is a hard hunter (he recently took a double grand slam of turkey during a single spring). In an effort to help those who are new to the intricacies of contest calling he has made and marketed a cassette tape that contains samples of his award winning turkey talk and a lot of good advice that can help any contest caller. ("Calling all Judges" can be ordered from Tony Kinton, P.O. Box 88, Carthage, MS 39051).

Eddie Salter of Evergreen, Alabama is a two time world champion contest caller who agrees that knowing the likes and dislikes of the judges can be a critical element in contest calling success. The preferences of contest calling judges can vary tremendously, Eddie says. Some like bell clear calls and others go for rasp. Much of the time the contestants do not know who the judges will be so they have no opportunity to "call to" individuals. Many regional calling contests, however, use the same general panel of judges time after time. A contestant should tape record a contest or two, listen to the recordings, and determine which kind of calls consistently score high.

Salter has been involved in competition calling for 12 years (as of 1990) and has won the world championship twice and finished one point out of first in 1990. His main mistake in early contests, he says, was in sounding too much like a turkey. He made many mistakes. Judges demand perfection and deduct points for each mistake, even very minor mistakes.

Eddie has a tendency, he feels, to hurry his calls. To compensate he writes a short message on the inside of his hand. "Take your time," the message reads, and it is repeated four times for empha-

World Champion turkey caller Eddie Salter has his own call company and is a popular seminar instructor.

sis. Eddie practices 45 minutes a day every day for the four or five weeks preceding a major contest.

The order the finalists appear is determined by a drawing. An early draw, say from one to five, can be deadly in Eddie's opinion. He recalls one contest where Eddie drew five and Dick Kirby drew three. Neither of these top notch callers scored highly enough to make it to the finals.

Competition calling offers many benefits. The contests offer the opportunity to fine tune calling skills during the off season. The contests offer each participant a chance to have his or her calls critiqued. There is the opportunity to have individual calling skills contrasted to the skills of others. Those few who have the talent and perserverence to consistently win accrue other rewards. Money, merchandise and fame, Every contestant, winner and loser alike, has fun. That alone, in the opinion of many, is reason enough to participate.

Wild turkey hens and toms seldom demand perfection in turkey talk. Contest judges almost always do.

73

THE TURKEY SCOUT
CHAPTER TEN

Pre-season scouting is the most important element in the successful hunting of the wild turkey. That statement applies equally to the spring and the fall seasons. If you do not know where the turkeys are, if you do not know a bit about their movement and routine, your chance of using your tag is slim.

Scouting out the spring turkey woods is less difficult than the fall scout. The birds are vocal in the spring and a hunter who uses his ears during the pre-dawn hour, uses his ears during that last hour that falls between dusk and dead dark, and uses his eyes in between, has a good chance of locating a turkey or turkeys.

Western hunters have an easier time scouting out a place to turkey hunt. Much of the land in the west, actually most of the land, is public land. Hunters there do not have the added worry of locating a land owner who will permit access. Much of the western lands, the habitat of the Merriam's sub-species mainly, is controlled by the National Forest Service (an agency of the United States Department of Agriculture), The Bureau of Land Management (Department of the Interior) or one of the state land departments. Much of this vast acreage of publicly owned land is managed for multiple use. Almost every acre has been mapped. Those maps can help the turkey hunter to take his tom. Maps of the national forests show numbered roads, waterholes, lakes and streams. The maps are color coded to indicate the approximate boundaries between public and private land. These maps are available at moderate price from the individual National Forest Offices. The appendix of this book will provide a listing of National Forest Headquarters and the address of each.

A more detailed map, a topographic map, is available from the U.S. Geological Survey. Topo maps are printed in a number of configurations but generally show a fairly small area of land in great detail. Elevation changes are indicated. So are some roads and some prominent geologic features. A listing of maps available can be obtained by writing to the U.S.G.S., Denver CO 80225 or the U.S.G.S., Washington, D.C., 20242. Maps can be ordered from the same two sources.

To make the best use of the topographic map spend a bit of time to become familiar with map symbols. Each topo map covers several square miles and elevation changes are indicated. Although the elevation scale may vary, contour lines very close together will indicate a steep ridge or a mountain. Public and private land is indicated. Roads are shown as primary, secondary and unimproved. Fences, field lines and water sources such as creeks, ponds and lakes are indicated.

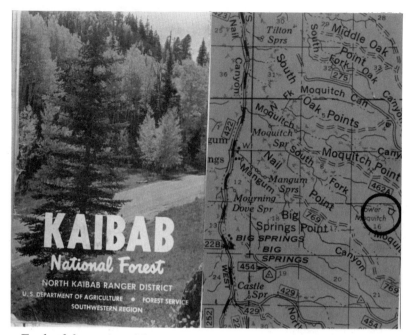

Each of the national forests issues a detailed map that is moderately priced. Consult the Appendix for a listing of national forests with addresses supplied for each.

Here are tips that may make your topo turkey hunting more successful.

Check the date the map was printed. Although it is not likely that major contour features will change, an out of date map may present an inaccurate representation of roads, fences, land ownership and water sources.

Consult the map scale and use a ruler to mark mileage in the area you intend to hunt. Take the map and a marking pen on the turkey scout to note changes.

If the map is badly outdated make local inquiry to learn of road changes. It can be frustrating to make a five mile predawn hike to hunt a wild area and find a four lane highway full of turkey hunters waiting when you arrive.

Use color coded marking pencils to mark places such as roosts, feeding, loafing areas, and places where you have heard gobbles.

Hunters scouting out western turkey country should locate water. Water is the limiting factor in much of the western turkey country and the birds will not be far away. A careful inspection will sometimes reveal tracks, droppings, lost feathers, strut marks or foraging scratches. Much of the western turkey land is leased to ranchers for summer graze. Cow plops are to be found in great number. (Particularly as you make that predawn crawl). The turkeys have learned that many kinds of delicious bugs set up housekeeping under the plops. A flock on the hunt for protein will use their beaks to flip the plops to get at the bugs who live on the small amount of moisture on the bottom side. Finding such an area can indicate the presence of turkey.

Western streams, and the green grass that borders the water, can attract turkeys.

Other animals, skunks and sometimes ravens, will at times utilize the same hunting technique but will usually do so in a greatly reduced area.

The roost tree of choice for much of the western turkey's range is the ponderosa pine tree. Look for live trees, not dead trees, and look for trees that are fully mature, the yellowbarks. Flocks of turkeys look for a grove of roost trees and not a single tree. It is uncommon for these turkeys to crowd together into a single tree. The flock will instead, scatter out among a group of trees that may extend for several hundred feet. This fact can be important to know if you setup on a roosted tom before daylight. Although your setup may be a safe distance away from the tom you may be directly beneath one of his hens. If she spooks he spooks.

77

Turkey hunters who hunt areas composed mostly of privately owned land have an added problem, that of obtaining access permission. The best time to do this is well before the spring or fall season opens. Permission is more easily obtained if the hunter and the landowner can find an area of common ground. A relative or perhaps a friend. Maybe even a common enemy. Do what is needed to convince the property owner that you are a responsible hunter who will treat the owner's land and property with proper respect.

The pre-season scout made by hunters in all areas of the country will be more productive if the hunter has the knowledge needed to properly interpret the sign that he sees. Droppings, feathers and tracks can tell the hunter much about the turkey that left the sign.

The track of an adult turkey gobbler is almost always larger than the track of a hen or an immature turkey. The middle toe of an adult gobbler is usually more than 2 1/2" long. The middle toe of a large hen will usually be less than 2 1/2" long. Carry a small lightweight tape measure to verify the measurement.

Gobblers are larger than hens and take a longer stride. The stride of a mature tom averages about eight inches. The stride of an average hen is about an inch less. The tracks left by running turkeys naturally show an increased stride. The toes will be spread and toenail indentations will be deep.

Western toms have big feet. The shell is a 10 gauge 3 1/2" magnum.

Midwestern, western and southwestern turkeys seem to have larger feet, and leave larger tracks, than do the turkey of the East and the South.

The droppings of the wild turkey can tell the sex of the pooper, the age, and at times how long ago the dirty deed was accomplished. If the dropping is not utterly ancient, the dropping can also provide a general idea of diet.

The dropping of adult gobblers are big boogers and are semi-straight, some having a small "J" curve at one end or sometimes slightly twisted. Hen droppings cluster together into an insipid looking glob, a tightly compacted corkscrew. Hen droppings are almost always smaller in diameter than gobbler droppings.

In some areas of the arid Southwest, places where a rain makes the front page of the paper, turkey droppings dry out quickly and last for a long time. A dropping that is a week old, many times, will look exactly the same as a dropping that is a month old. A wet or semi-wet dropping usually indicates that a turkey was close by within the last day or so. A wet dropping indicates that, unless it rained the night before the scout was made.

Fall turkeys east and west seek out mast crops like these acorns.

In Eastern turkey range, where rain is more frequent, droppings from turkeys who have fed on soft foods such as berries may disappear quickly. Other droppings, made of more durable stuff such as mast, seeds and grass, contain little moisture and will stay intact much longer.

Every feather on a turkey's body is discarded at least one time during a period of one year. Turkeys travel several miles each day and leave many tracks. And if the grocery supply is good, a turkey will poop a couple of dozen times each day. That adds up to a lot of sign.

Western hunters can often obtain information on turkey sightings by talking to those who spend a good deal of their time in the woods. Ranchers and those who work for the ranchers can be good sources. So are forest service employees and game and fish guys.

Turkeys can become burnt out on crow and owl calls. Sounding something different, like a predator distress scream, sometimes works.

Those who hunt east of the West might find that the owner of the land where they have permission to hunt will be the best source of information on turkey sightings. Others who drive the roads regularly, folks like the rural mail carrier, the drivers of delivery trucks, even school bus drivers, can report turkey sightings unless they happen to also hunt turkeys. In that event, forget it. Any information revealed is likely to be inaccurate.

Spring gobblers often gobble just before daylight to announce their location to the hens. One gobble will generally trigger a second, and soon every turkey tom within hearing will sound off. Mature toms also gobble shortly after fly up near dark, although these dusk and dead dark gobbles are seldom as enthusiastic and numerous.

Don't mess around with the turkeys you locate on the scout as the experience will educate them to the call.

Every gobbler does not perform his vocal advertisement at dawn and dusk on every day. On some days Rambo could not make a turkey gobble using an assault rifle. On other days every turkey in the woods will gobble enthusiastically each time a cricket chirps.

Mature male turkeys gobble for a number of reasons in the spring. They gobble primarily, in likelihood, as an advertisement. The gobble tells the hen the location of the turkey equivalent of a hunk. The hen hears, and if she does not have a headache, yelps out an answer and moves toward the tom. The tom, if he does not already have plenty of hens, may move toward the hen. They meet at some point and the gobbler does his little dance on the hen's back.

The spring tom may also gobble as a territorial announcement. He is telling other toms that a certain Robert Redford McTurk has set up shop within a certain area and will vigorously defend that territory against all intruders.

An early morning crow call will sometimes cause a tom to shock gobble.

Male turkeys will sometimes gobble enthusiastically as a response to any and all unexpected sounds. Some spring birds will gobble each time a thunder clap occurs. Or he may gobble in response to an owl hoot, a crow call, a hawk scream, a coyote howl or an elk bugle. Turkeys at times will gobble their heads off when they hear a car door slam. This "shock" gobbling helps the hunter. He or she can carefully listen as they scout the turkey woods. A number of devices are available to simulate the sounds that most often prompt the shock gobble. Hunters can scout by walking the woods or driving the roads, stopping frequently to vocalize on or more gobble producing sound.

In heavy hunted areas (or heavy scouted areas) turkeys are apt to become educated to the most often used sounds. Getting a gobble out of one of these jaded birds is difficult. They have heard so many owl hoots and crow calls that they can often tell both the kind of call the hunter is using and perhaps even the brand name and pattern on his camo.

Spring gobblers will also respond to a wide variety of turkey talk at times. The yelp of a hen, made near the peak gobbling periods of dawn and dusk, is likely to elicit a response. If you use a hen yelp to get a gobble while on a pre- hunt scout do not get carried away with the fun of it all and continue to talk to that turkey until he wears out his gobble. It is best to make a notation that logs his location and then quietly leave the area. Too much talk to the turkey before the season begins can cause that turkey to be a hard sell when you come back to work him on opening day.

Do not assume that gobble prompters such as hooters, crow calls and even yelpers will cause a gobbler to sound off each time he hears one. That is not the case. The author was on a hunt for Merriams during the 1990 spring and had found fresh turkey sign near a meadow. The area offered all a turkey needed. Food, a nearby water supply, and plenty of roost trees. The author and his companion parked a mile away well before dawn the next morning and made the cold hike into the area. Hard work with the hooter (making the call of the Great Horned Owl) produced no results. A coyote howl worked no better. Convinced that a turkey had to be in that area, a setup was established and a few tentative yelps were sounded. The nearby woods exploded with gobbles from at least three turkeys.

Telemetry studies have indicated that spring turkeys in all parts of their range do not move great distances during a day unless there is a need. In good habitat, an area that holds plenty of turkey food, water and roost trees, the hunk and his harem may spend the entire day within a somewhat small geographic area.

It is good strategy to scout out more than one gobbler during a pre-hunt foray. On public land particularly, a turkey hunter who has bet all the marbles on a single gobbler may find that he has a lot of company on opening day. The roadside near "his" gobbler might resemble the main parking lot at the county fair. Having back up birds makes sense.

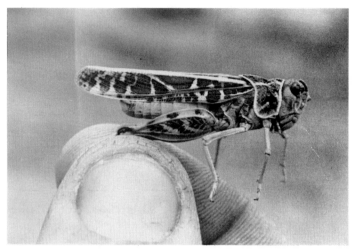

Late spring hunters look for grasshoppers that may attract protein hungry turkey.

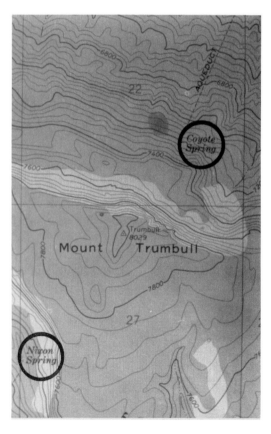

Topo maps show springs (circled) and elevation changes.

Pre-hunt scouting offers a number of advantages to the turkey hunter. Birds are located, the hunter can set out before dawn on opening morning confident that he has a roosted bird to work, or at the very least, know that he will be hunting in an area that shows turkey activity. Pre-hunt scouting also allows the hunter to learn the lay of the land. Locating creeks, fences and other obstacles that can cause a turkey to hang up can be valuable knowledge when it comes time to work a turkey. Finally, the prehunt scout tells the hunter something about turkey movements. Turkeys are birds of habit. If they work their way to water shortly after flydown on a Tuesday they are likely to do exactly the same, taking the same path, on Wednesday. The hunter who scouts his or her hunting area before the season opens has a leg up on the competition. That advantage will many times translate to a successful hunt.

The mud that borders ponds can display sign that suggests turkey activity, number of birds using water, sex and frequency of visit.

The five sub-species of the wild turkey are essentially identical in appearance even though there are subtle variations in feather color. If each of the sub-species lived in identical terrain the flock habits would closely correspond. The turkeys do not live in identical terrain, however, and some do not even live in similar terrain. The mesquite dotted grasslands of south Texas, home to the Rio Grande, is far different from either the hardwood habitat of the Eastern or the mature ponderosa pine lands that house the Merriams. The habitat occupied by the wild turkey has influenced habit. The Eastern turkey who prowls the hardwood forest of Pennsylvania or Missouri, honed by hunter pressure, can react to a call differently from a transplanted Merriams of Kansas or Iowa who has virgin ears. Turkey hunters who travel to hunt give away the home field advantage. The following paragraphs provide an insight into the technique used by high profile hunters to take tough spring turkeys in their neck of the woods.

Dick Kirby is a master turkey hunter who has matched wits with "the Eastern" gobblers many times, in his home state of New York and in many other states. His passion for wild turkey hunting meshes comfortably with his position as owner of Quaker Boy Calls, a manufacturer of quality turkey calls. The birds that Dick remembers best are the really tough turkeys, the birds that caused him to dredge up every but of his turkey hunting skill. Those difficult birds, Dick feels, give him added insight into the nature of the wild turkey. The Rio Grande bird Dick tagged in Oklahoma during the 1986 season is an example.

"I was there about two weeks too late to make the breeding peak," he recalls, "and was having a hard time." To make matters worse strong winds, an Oklahoma "breeze", made it difficult for Dick to hear the turkeys and for the turkeys to hear Dick. A call that might arouse a gobbler a mile away on a less windy day would die two hundred yards out. Dick switched to the box, depending on the extra volume to fight out a bit further. Finally, faint and far away, came the answer he hoped for.

A second gobble a minute or so later was closer. The tom was on his way. Dick made a fast setup and made one more call. The gobbler answered but because of the wind sounded to be farther away than he was. Dick rose to move closer. Halfway up he sighted a bobbing white head coming his way. He dropped back and got hid.

The gobbler came close but made a turn that put him away from the gun. He was too close to try a quick draw. Dick used a trick he has used many times on spooky gobblers. He soft called with the diaphragm he held in his mouth. In an instant the tom turned around. He wheeled, putting his fanned tail to the gun. Dick used that time to get on target. When the tom completed the turn he found himself looking into the awesome bore of a Mag-Ten.

Master turkey hunter Dick Kirby keeps moving to take windy day gobblers. (Photo from Mr. Kirby's files).

The trick to windy day hunting, according to Dick Kirby, is to keep on the move. Setting up to call from a constant location does little good. The wind kills the call and a small amount of area is covered. Moving permits the call to cover a lot more territory.

How you call on windy days can be important. Volume is important. The box is a good call because it broadcasts a loud message. And Dick Kirby really cranks down on it. Sooner or later, he says, the loud yelps will elicit a response from a windy day gobbler. When you have had the chance to pinpoint his location (often more difficult because of the wind) and move to a set up, you can work that gobbler just as you would work any other gobbler.

Kelly Cooper, a world champion turkey caller and another hard hunter who has his own call company calls Picture Rocks, Pennsylvania his home. Kelly has worked more tough turkey than he can count. Like Kirby, Kelly likes to keep moving as he tries to locate a tom. But Kelly does it on calm days as well as windy days. Float calling he calls it.

There are a lot more turkey hunters now than in years past. That increase in numbers has caused Pennsylvania turkey to become more sophisticated and less responsive to a call. "In the old days," Kelly recalls, "I could drive the back roads to caw or owl, locate a roosted bird, and go back in the morning and have a fair chance of calling him in. That is no longer true."

Kelly Cooper imitates a hen in both calls and movement to work tough turkey.
Kelly Cooper Photo.

Kelly gives an example. He located a tom by driving the road and stopping frequently to give locator calls. He went home happy and was in position to work the bird before daylight the next morning. "I really had that bird going, he was gobbling and double gobbling. Suddenly a truck motor purred to a stop 200 yards away and a hunter began working a box. The gobbler did not respond. The hunter on the road switched to a gobble hose and then a hooter. The tom stayed mute. The tom had shutmouth so bad you couldn't have pried his mouth open with a crowbar. After ten minutes the hunter left. Two minutes after that the bird began to gobble on his own. Lesson? Turkeys are harder hunted now and are more sophisticated about road calling. A hunter who hopes to score consistently must leave the road. That is where float calling comes in."

Most hard hunters know that calling a tom to a hen call is causing that turkey to go against his nature. Normally the hen goes to the tom. The natural hen seldom stays in one spot for 45 minutes to make seductive yelps, as the imitation hen does. That fact can send a danger signal to an educated tom. When float calling, Kelly Cooper moves to the tom, just as a genuine hen would move as she feeds and dawdles her way to the tom. Kelly works as close to the tom as he safely can and then sets up. "By this time," Kelly says, "the bird is so hot he comes at a dead run."

Here is the way Kelly Cooper normally hunts a spring tom. He studies topo maps to pick an area to hunt. Nearly thirty years of hunting experience have provided an insight into the territory turkey prefer and Kelly concentrates on those areas.

Before daylight on the day of the hunt he parks his truck a safe distance away and walks into the area listening for turkey sounds. If none are heard Kelly makes soft clucks and yelps as he moves. Eventually a gobbler will respond. When that happens Kelly goes into the float calling mode. He moves to the gobble five or ten steps and calls again. He varies the direction of travel, calling from each new position. He may even back up twenty five yards. The goal is to make the tom think that Kelly is a real hen, one that is interested but not easy. It will not be long before the gobbler is so hot he might try to kiss a bobcat. Careful listening will tell when the gobbler has had enough. When he can't stand it any more and comes at a run. This is the time to make a fast set up and be ready when the gobbler shows.

Moving around as Kelly does when float calling can spook any turkey that spots the movement. Kelly knows that and takes the risk. More often, the technique works to excite a tough turkey that might not otherwise respond. And taking one of those sophisticated turkeys, according to Kelly Cooper, makes the risks involved worthwhile.

Bill Harper of Neosho, Missouri has a different way of working toms who have heard too many exquisitely articulated yelps, clucks and purrs. Harper, as nearly everyone knows, is a hard hunter who has owned a game call manufacturing company (Lohman/Bill Harper), a man who has hunted turkeys and other wildlife from coast to coast. Bill's years of experience hunting and studying the wild turkey have provided a rare insight into the turkey personality. This insight was demonstrated a number of times when the author joined Bill on a turkey hunt that took place in a hard hunted public land area in eastern Oklahoma, but was illustrated particularly well when a longbeard used his long legs to dart across a county road in front of Bill's vehicle.

Bill Harper hoots to locate early day gobblers.

Before the running tom could reach the brushline that bordered the road Bill slowed, stuck his head out of the van window, and used his natural voice to gobble out a challenge. The big bronzeback stopped in midstep, hesitated an instant, and went into a full strut gobbling his patriotic head off. Surprise a turkey, Bill explained, by doing something unexpected and they will respond as their nature suggests.

The Oklahoma turkeys were a hard sell. They had heard owl hoots and crow caws until they were sick of them. Bill reached into his experience to find the technique that would restore vigor to these tired turkeys. It was time for Bill and hunting companion Ronnie Conner to try the hard sell.

Bill drove the vehicle through the back roads looking for likely turkey country. Maybe the point of a ridge that led from a mountain rim to a meadow, or down to water. When such a spot was found one of the two would use a mouth diaphragm (Lohman/Bill Harper 836) to produce a series of cutts and cackles that would warm the heart of the most jaded gobbler. When a gobbler boomed out an answer, Bill or Ronnie, or both, would hurry out to set up on the tom to work him in.

Hooting with a hooter can be effective but calls do not have volume of natural voice hoots.

Every tom that gobbled at the cutting and cackling did not come to the call. Some turned shut mouth. Others, obviously with hens, were all talk and no walk. Some turkeys, bless 'em, came with enthusiasm. One got so carried away he tried to mate with Wicked Wanda, Bill's beat up hen turkey decoy.

The most reliable spring tactic in any part of the country is the tried and true "roost 'em at night and work them at daylight" tactic. The turkeys can be located in a number of different ways.

Some hunters find a high point in good turkey country and set up there about an hour before dead dark. The hunter does nothing but listen, hoping to hear a tom gobble out a good night as he curls his toes around the roost limb. When a gobble is heard the hunter notes location as best he can, uses a flashlight to return to his vehicle, and sets up somewhat close to the tom the next morning.

Other hunters drive back roads or walk through turkey country using a locator call to try to prompt a shock gobble. The hunter notes the location of the gobble (or gobbles) and comes back to work the bird before daylight.

Others use boxes, wingbones, slates or diaphragms to make turkey talk (mostly simple yelps) as they travel through turkey country. When gobblers are located they mark the location and return the next morning for the set up.

There is a danger in talking turkey to a roosted tom. Many times the tom will lock in on the source of that yelp with enthusiastic anticipation. There is a fifty-fifty chance he will head for that hen yelp at flydown the next morning, even if the hunter is set up right under the roost sending out some of the most delightful turkey sounds ever heard. Hunters can compensate for this tendency by setting up between the gobbler and the source of the locator yelp made the night before.

Turkey hunters of limited experience sometimes have a problem in deciding exactly how to work a roosted tom. They become confused at times about the basics of set up and the kind of calls to use. Turkeys are individuals and a technique that works well on one might work less well on another. The geography of the roost site can have an influence on the proper way to make the setup. Here are generalized tactics that might work.

Park the vehicle as far away from the roost as practical. A half mile or more is not too far. Make the walk in by moonlight or starlight if possible. If not, use a low power flashlight only when needed.

Get to within one hundred yards of the roosted bird if you can do so without risking discovery. Remember that gobblers often roost with hens and they are likely to be in different trees. You may be a

safe distance from the gobbler but be so close that you frighten the hen. If you spook the hen you have likely spooked the gobbler. It is better to be too far away than to be too close.

Get into your setup at least one half hour before first light. Scouting trips have likely provided information on the precise time the dark begins to fade. You should be settled into your setup before first light.

Pick a tree wider than your back for the setup. This will break your outline and will provide protection if a too eager hunter comes back door. Remove all sticks and rocks that are irritants immediately to avoid squirming around later as the discomfort becomes acute. Select a sitting position you can maintain for at least an hour if need be. Most experienced hunters sit with their back supported against a tree with legs either straight out or flexed at the knees.

Lay out the calls you will be using beside you so that it will not be necessary to fumble in your pockets or fanny pack at an inopportune time.

Your gun should have been loaded as you left the vehicle. Check to be sure the safety is on (do not do this by pulling on the trigger) and position the gun so that it is available. Some hunters feel comfortable with the gun leaned against one leg. Other like to lay it across their lap. Do what is comfortable to you.

Pull on face net and camo gloves. Settle in and wait for the gobbler or one of the hens with him to make the first move.

Turkeys, both hens and toms, are vocal at daylight. If hens are present you will hear "tree talk", low volume yelps, clucks and purrs. If the gobbler has not already gobbled, he probably will do so at this time.

Some gobblers begin gobbling while it is dead dark. It is probably best to ignore such a blabbermouth. There is no chance the bird will fly down while it is dark. Talking to the bird accomplishes no useful purpose. Wait until the dark starts to fade, when flydown becomes a possibility, and let the gobbler know (in a subtle way) that you are close by and with a bit of encouragement can be had.

When you are close to a turkey it is best to call as little as possible. Announce your presence by making two or three soft clucks, yelps or purrs. Then shut up. The gobbler keeps his lust sated by listening for those exact sounds, keying in on them, and responding. If he has no hens, and no better prospects, that meager amount of calling will likely bring him close for a look.

If you hear the gobbler fly down and hear other turkeys fly down, and if you have heard only one gobbler, it is nearly certain the tom has hens with him. If those birds move away from your setup and the gobbler stays vocal, talk to him frugally. No amount of calling is likely to call him away from the hens. It is likely, however, that he will return to check you out when his cluster of hens have been serviced and they wander off to nest or to locate a nest site. Do not succumb to temptation and attempt to follow the flock or to intercept them. Such attempts are seldom successful and usually result in alarming the birds, consequently reducing your chances of calling the tom in when the hens depart.

When a gobbler flies down with hens let them leave and work the gobbler when the hens leave to nest.

If you hear only one flydown and the gobbler develops shut-mouth when he hits the ground, or if he gobbles a time or two and then develops lockjaw, do not become dismayed. That gobbler, in all probability, is standing at attention just out of sight, doing his best to determine if you are in fact a turkey. Wait that turkey out and do so with a minimum of calling (maybe none). Patience is a deadly weapon to use against a turkey and has likely killed more longbeards than all of the fancy techniques combined. How long should you wait? An hour is not too long. If you wait that long send out frugal yelps every ten minutes or so.

If a turkey responds to your calling but hangs up out of gun range try the patience technique on him also. Birds of this type will frequently gobble their heads off, applauding every call you make, but will not come one step toward the setup. The bird may be hung up for a number of reasons. There may be a physical obstacle (or something that the bird perceives to be an obstacle) between you and the bird. Turkeys will sometimes hang up because of fences, streams or any other aberration that might confuse his love starved brain. Your knowledge of the area might supply an answer. If not, you may need to move on the tom but should try another technique first.

Turkeys sometimes hang up because they are not solidly convinced it is safe to proceed. He may have had a bad experience with your brand of turkey call very recently. Or there may be something about your setup (too brushy) that urges caution. If you are hunting with a companion, try this. You or your companion sneak away from the turkey fifty or one hundred yards, yelping disappointedly along the way. This tells the turkey that the hot hen is cooling off and may leave the country. Many hung up toms will move in response to the tactic and the hunter left behind, the gunner, will have his shot.

Obstacles and perceived obstacles can cause a turkey to hang up.

If the "I'm getting the hell out of here" ploy does not work try another. If you are sure it is safe to do so, if you are convinced that no other hunter is nearby, use a gobbler call to tell the tom that some other hunk is attempting to have his way with the hen. If it is a two hunter setup, or if you are coordinated enough to shake a gobble tube and yelp on a diaphragm at the same time, such double calling is sometimes effective.

As a last resort, move on the hung up gobbler. Do not move straight to him. He will be watching for the hesitant hen and will immediately recognize that you are not her. Sneak away from the gobbler a safe distance and make a circling maneuver that takes you to his far side. Do not call as you make this sneak. Try to place yourself about a hundred yards on his far side (if practical) and make another setup. If a buddy is along leave him or her at the original setup. There will be times when the hung up gobbler runs for that spot like a racehorse as soon as he thinks you have abandoned it.

The most difficult turkey to take, much of the time, is the turkey tom who absolutely will not gobble. If you know there is a longbeard in the area, and repeated calls go unanswered, try the stingy box technique. Set up and rake out meager yelps, perhaps three yelps each 15 minutes, and stay on the stand for a minimum of two hours. There will be times, quite often actually, when the silent tom will come sneaking in to take a look. Frugal calling and patience are a deadly combination.

Spring turkeys are fun to hunt but are not easy to hunt. The hunter who has patience, determination and a bit of calling skill has an advantage. The hunter can make a hundred mistakes. The turkey can make only one.

Strong wind can make it hard for the turkey to hear the hunter and hard for the hunter to hear the turkey.

THE FALL HUNT
CHAPTER TWELVE

The fall turkey is different from the spring turkey. The turkey flocks are segregated by sex and by age. The long bearded gobblers are clustered into bachelor bands bonded by a common interest. Finding enough food to keep their big bodies healthy enough to last a potentially severe winter. Banded, they are able to forage more efficiently and more safely. Many pairs of eyes are able to discover danger more quickly than a single pair.

The hens stay with their poults. Several hens and their jennies may join to form multi-family groups. The jakes, young males of the year, are likely off in bands of their own. Bigger than the young hens, bigger even than the brood hen, jakes are unwelcome additions to either hen bands or the mature gobbler bands. The jake's teenage attempts at dominance have forced him away from the brood hen. His inexperience at the serious job of survival causes him to be equally unwelcome with the gobbler. Too old to be a dependent and too young to be an asset to adult toms, the jakes wander about in teenage bands, gathering the experience needed to be a successful wild turkey tom.

A fresh snow can be a boon to the fall turkey hunter hoping to locate turkeys.

Fall turkey flocks are not nearly as vocal as spring flocks. There is no reason for the mature toms to gobble repeatedly to advertise their whereabouts to potentially receptive hens. Some jake turkeys, and some adult males, gobble in the fall even though there is no good reason, but the jake flocks and the gobbler bands are essentially mute, making only those small noises needed to maintain contact with other flock members.

Hen flocks are somewhat more vocal than the tom bands but are much more discrete than they will be during the spring. This lack of language causes the birds to be difficult to locate and difficult to hunt.

Fall turkey hunters must depend on other evidence to assist them in their search for wild turkey flocks. The size of the wild turkey, and the way they make their living, can cause a lot of clues to be left for those astute enough to profit from them.

Fall turkeys move about a great deal, probably more so than spring turkeys. A flock can leave a lot of tracks. A skilled woodsman can determine the direction of travel, how long ago the turkeys travelled by, and the sexual composition of the flock by examining the tracks. "Generations" of tracks can reveal if the travelway is one that is used on a somewhat routine basis. Tracks can also supply information that can lead to an educated guess about the number of turkeys in the flock.

Dropped feathers and droppings can also tell a story. The sex of the individual turkey can be discovered by either feather or dropping. A number of shed feathers or droppings concentrated in a small area may indicate a roost. Partially digested food items in the droppings can indicate major fall foods and provide a clue to feeding grounds. Dusting depressions can indicate areas where the flock shades up to escape the sometimes warm fall sun.

Fall turkeys can be successfully hunted using a variety of technique. The most exciting is likely the popular "scatter and call back" system. An efficient scatter can provide a wonderful opportunity to call the birds to the gun in much the way that spring birds are called.

The scatter can be accomplished in several ways. Some hunters locate a roosting area and rush in to scatter the roosted birds just before flydown. Others locate turkeys along a travelway, on a food ground, or in a loafing area and rush in to make the scatter. If the birds fly off in one direction you have succeeded in scaring the hell out of a flock of turkeys but you have not made a scatter. A successful scatter sees the birds depart in many directions.

Some sophisticated fall hunters have trained dogs (not legal in all areas) to do the scattering. The trained dog is turned out to hunt in good turkey country and ranges until a flock of turkeys is located. The dog charges the flock barking excitedly. When the turkeys fly to scatter, the dog remains at the point of the scatter, barking to bring the hunters. A natural blind is constructed at the point and the hunter or hunters set up to call the birds back. The dog, if properly trained, will lay quietly in the blind until the action is ended.

Some states permit the use of turkey dogs during the fall hunt. The dogs do the hard work of finding the flocks and making the scatter, then sit quietly while the hunter attempts to call them back.

Flushed turkeys will not fly far if the land is flat, usually not much farther than the length of a football field or two. Turkey flocks scattered on a ridge may fly and soar much farther.

Wait at least 30 minutes before making an attempt to call the turkeys back to the flush site. It may take the birds that long to recover from the fright of the flush. The brood hen, much of the time, will be the first to return to the area of the scatter to sound the assembly call. Do not permit her to do this. The poults will recognize her yelps and will gather on her, even if you happen to be a competition class caller. Frighten the hen as far away as possible. Return to the blind and make an attempt to call in one or more of the young birds. Early in the fall season the jakes are likely to be mixed in with the hens and the jennies. Hunters who wish to do so may be able to select a young male bird for the table.

The most difficult part of the scatter/call fall technique is finding a flock to scatter and then affecting dispersal. All turkey flocks have likely been scattered a number of times, either by predators or by hunters. It is their nature to flush as a flock to facilitate reassembly. Effecting a decent dispersal puts the hunter in an advanta-

geous position. The gregarious birds are desperate to get back together and it is instinct to reassemble near the point of the flush. A
caller with only moderate calling skills can be successful.

*A successful scatter can cause that point to be a good place to call
from for several days.*

The younger flock members try to get back together by sounding the call humans have named the kee kee or the kee kee run. The birds are likely to become vocal about forty five minutes after the flush. Some hunters initiate the conversation by beginning to kee kee about a half hour after the flush. Much of the time a bird, or birds, will respond.

The best call to make is the call that the turkeys make. If you hear the distinctive four note call of the jake, repeat it. If you hear the kee kee run followed by a series of yelps that is characteristic of the jennies, repeat that. Call back each time the turkey calls to you. The hen is out there somewhere and will be calling to her flock some time soon. Try to get your bird close before she starts.

When a returning turkey comes close to the scatter site, to a point where he or she expects to see a turkey, they are likely to cluck. A sort of "where 'n hell are you, buddy?" Cluck back if you are well hid, but cluck reluctantly. It might be safer to remain mute. Better to be thought a fraud than to cluck and remove all doubt.

If the flock has been efficiently scattered, and you remain to take a returning turkey, that spot may be just as effective a place to call from later that same day or even on the next day. A panic dispersal sometimes makes reassembly difficult and time consuming. The brood hen may collect a part of her flock and depart, leaving the rest of the poults to get back to the flock the best way they can.

Separated fall turkeys are very vocal as they attempt reassembly and a fall hunter should be equally vocal. Decrease the amount and volume of the calls as the turkeys come close.

The ambush is a fall turkey technique that has put many a tasty young bird on Thanksgiving table. Western hunters who hunt the southwestern range of the Merriams and the Rio Grande subspecies often set up on a trail that leads to water. Those who hunt areas where water is available in many places set up on travelways that lead from the roost grounds to the feed grounds. Western hunters, where the rifle continues to be considered an honorable way to take a turkey, often use binoculars to glass open country hoping to discover a turkey or a flock of turkeys. When birds are located the hunter approaches to decent rifle range and uses a scope sighted centerfire rifle to make the kill.

Calling to a roosted flock at about flydown can be a productive way to take a fall turkey. Some fall turkey hunters remember favored roosting areas from years past and will visit those areas in the evening to listen for fly ups. When a roost is located they return before daylight the next morning, just as they would do in the spring season, and set up to call to the birds.

Roost calling can be a good technique to facilitate the taking of a super smart fall gobbler. It has been said that it is nearly impossible to overcall to a fall turkey and that is probably true. The exception to that rule is a fall gobbler. Unlike his spring counterpart, mature toms are the strong silent type in the fall. They do not vocalize a lot and don't like to hang around with turkeys that do. Call sparingly to a roosted tom. Toss him a cluck. If he answers the cluck respond with three or four coarse gobbler yelps. Then shut up. If the tom is interested he will sneak in for a quick look.

What about scattering a bachelor band of fall toms and setting up to call them back? That can be tough to do. The bond that holds fall toms together can be tenuous. There is not a desperate compulsion to regroup. The regrouping, much of the time, is accidental as the toms wander the woods. The toms do deliberately regroup at times but do so leisurely, sometimes taking several days to do so.

Coarse yelps to a roosted tom can cause a fall longbeard to sneak in for a look.

Fall hunting regulations, almost always, permit taking a bird of either sex. The hen that is protected during the spring hunt is put at risk during the fall hunt. Why is this so? Studies in Arkansas have shown that many of those fall birds will not see the first flower of spring. Predation will cause many to disappear. Winter kill will take others. The bird tagged on a fall hunt, whether it be gobbler, jake, brood hen or jennie, is not likely to make it through the winter in any case.

Hunters who desire personalized instruction in fall calls and fall hunting techniques should consider the purchase of a cassette or video. Kelly Kallers (P.O.Box 49, Kelly Lane, Picture Rocks, PA 17762) has an excellent cassette titled Fall Turkey Hunting Strategy. The tape explains tactics and demonstrates fall calls that have worked for this hard hunter.

Fall Turkey Hunting, is a high quality video produced and marketed by Denny Gulvas (Gulvas Wildlife Adventures, RD #3, Box 235-B, DuBois, PA 15801). Gulvas, a four time winner of the prestigious U.S. Open calling championship, shares the fall calling and hunting technique that has made him a very successful hunter.

The fall hunt, even though it does not usually deliver the same excitement of a spring hunt, can be fine. The autumn woods are breathtaking in their beauty. There is a thing in the frosty fall air that causes a hunter's heart to ache to be afield. And the fall turkey, exactly like his or her spring counterpart, can be mighty tasty on the table.

Run the brood hen off if she is the first to return after a scatter.
Photo: Bureau of Sports Fisheries & Wildlife.

OUT OF STATE HUNTS
CHAPTER THIRTEEN

Turkey hunters are the most fortunate of hunters in many ways. They are fortunate because they possess the determination and skill to match wits with the magnificent wild turkey, a bird that is so large he is classified as big game in many states. The turkey hunter, unlike nearly all other hunters, has the opportunity to hunt two times a year, once in the spring and again in the fall. And finally, the dedicated turkey hunter is offered the opportunity to travel to near or far away states to expand his turkey hunting opportunities. Non-resident licenses for the turkey hunt, unlike most other big game, can be purchased at moderate cost.

Hunters from Kansas, Wisconsin and Arizona display the fine Rio Grande turkeys taken during the 1990 spring season in Kansas. Author is at right.

Hunters who have the time and the funds can find good turkey hunting somewhere during the spring season for approximately two and a half months. The State of Hawaii opens their spring season about the first of March. Many of the southern states open spring turkey season ten days later. Many western states end their season during the latter part of May. Both *The Turkey Hunter* magazine (Krause Publications, 700 East State Street, Iola Wisconsin, 54990) and *Turkey Call*, the magazine of the National Wild Turkey Federation (P.O. Box 530, Edgefield, S.C, 29824) publish spring and fall hunting guides that list season state by state.

Out of state hunts can be arranged in one of three ways. The cold turkey drop-in drive-in is one and is undoubtedly the worst. This involves driving day and night to a neighboring state and working desperately to line up a place to hunt turkeys before dead dark of a Sunday night. Not much fun and seldom productive.

A better way is the buddy hunt. A hunter in one state contacts a hunter in the target state and writes or calls to say something like this. "Hey Bubba. I hanker to hunt Alabama. If you can point me in the direction of good turkey woods I surenhek will return the favor when you come to Missouri."

How does one locate the "buddy"? If you have relatives in the target state talk to them to see if there is a turkey hunting cousin hid away in Possum Holler. If you are not that lucky ask the relative to supply the name and address of a local hunter.

A second way to locate an out of state buddy is to advertise in a magazine such as *The Turkey Hunter*. A few bucks will buy a classified advertisement that lists your wants and lists what you have to trade. The trade need not always be turkey for turkey. A hunter in South Dakota, for example, might offer a quality ringneck pheasant hunt in exchange for a similar quality turkey hunt in a state like Arizona where pheasants are few and far between.

The third out of state option may be the best although admittedly it is the most expensive. This option involves contracting for a guided or non-guided hunt at one of the turkey hunting lodges located in a high turkey density areas. The price paid will be dependent on the amount of services offered. A fully guided hunt at one of the luxury lodges, with bed and board included, might eat up the best part of a thousand dollar bill. At the other end of the economic spectrum a bare bones hunt that provides only access to a good turkey hunting area might run as low as fifty dollars a day. Both types of facilities, and others that occupy a more middle ground, regularly advertise in both *The Turkey Hunter* and *Turkey Call.*

To get the most out of an out of state hunt it is necessary to do a bit of pre-planning. A letter or a telephone call to the fish and game guys within the target state (telephone numbers and addresses are listed in the state guides mentioned later) will yield up current information on non-resident fees, season dates, and interesting intricacies of the regulations. What intricacies? The State of New Mexico, as an example, has regulated areas where two turkeys are allowed each spring and other areas that offer only one turkey each spring. Knowing that fact can be a help when it comes time to select a hunting area. Want another? Missouri has a split spring season. One gobbler is allowed during each one of those seasons. Plan your hunt to coincide with the end of the first season and the start of the second season and you can double your hunting pleasure at about the same price. Other states, Oklahoma and Alabama come immediately to mind, offer multiple turkey tags but restrict the take to no more than one turkey each day. Knowing of this before your plans are set in concrete can be a help in deciding where you want to hunt and when you want to hunt.

A request to the target state can bring good information on hunt options and equipment needed. Mark Kayser - S.D. Dept. of Tourism.

It is sometimes best, if the target state is somewhat close to your home, to drive to the hunting area. Taking your own vehicle permits you to carry along all of the gear turkey hunters accumulate, provides transportation at the destination, and can even provide a place to sleep (or carry camping gear) if equipped with a camper or a camper shell.

If the hunting destination is distant, and if time is a factor, airline travel might be the sensible way to go. Most of the major airlines, maybe even all, know the federal regulations as they apply to the air transportation of firearms and ammunition. Basically, the gun must be packed in a sturdy locked container that will protect it during some potentially rough treatment. The gun must be unloaded and much of the time the airline baggage clerk will insist on a personal inspection to verify that fact. No ammunition can be included in the same case that holds the gun. Both gun and ammo must be declared at the time you check your baggage. The clerk attaches a tag to the gun case that reads somewhat as follows: "I understand that the carriage of a loaded weapon is a violation of federal regulations. I therefore declare that the firearm contained in my luggage is not loaded and my luggage contains no more than five pounds of ammunition per firearm transported. Furthermore the luggage containing the declared firearm(s) is locked and I alone am in possession of the key or combination." You are asked to sign your name to the declaration and the cased gun is whisked away.

A pickup carrying a camper can provide transportation and lodging on low budget hunts.

It is good policy, probably, to be at the carousel at the time your cased gun is spit out at the other end. Cased guns are distinctive and are obviously an item of some value. There is a temptation here for thievery and there are thieves about.

There are a number of gun cases on the market sturdy enough to protect a gun during travel. Author has used the Browning (Route One, Morgan Utah 84050-9749) Gun Vault and found it to be big enough to hold two guns, and strong enough to protect both from every threat excepting a deliberate attack from a D-8 Caterpillar equipped with tungsten tipped rippers.

The Kolpin Gun Boot (123 S. Pearl Street, Berlin WI 54923) is another good one and is available at a bargain price. The gun boot, however, is a single gun carrier.

Some preplanning is needed to decide how the trophy or trophies will be transported home. Hunters who drive need only place the plucked bird in a cool chest, surround it with wet or dry ice, and head homeward. If the bird is to be mounted it will be transported in much the same way but will not be plucked. Protect the feathers from the water created by melting ice. Put the bird into a large (30 gallon size) trash bag, tie the top shut, and lay the package on the ice.

Hunters who fly to and from the hunt have a tougher time. It is best to have the carcass frozen if facilities are available. The frozen bird can be then be placed in an inexpensive styrofoam ice chest, taped shut, and then checked just as any other luggage will be checked.

Eastern hunters who come west will find a four wheel drive vehicle to be an asset.

Spend a good deal of the prehunt planning time considering hunting options and hunting equipment. The booking of one guide, on occasion, can lead to hunts in multiple states. A hunter who books to hunt Merriams in the Black Hills of South Dakota, as an example, can ask that same outfitter to provide hunts in the nearby states of Montana and Wyoming. Three turkey hunts for little more than the price of one is a bargain in anyone's ballpark.

The equipment needed to hunt turkey should be so obvious that it does not need explanation. It is not so. Differing terrains can cause a dramatic change in equipment needs. An Arizona hunter (author) once journeyed to Alabama to pursue the wily Eastern turkey. That hunter took along his dryland Redwing boots, a pair that had seldom felt a drop of rain. The 'bama hunt involved a march through a swamp that nearly sucked the boots from the hunter's feet. Oh for a pair of hipboots or waders.

That same hunter, on that same trip, was introduced to thousands (perhaps millions) of mosquitos who saw his big body as a smorgasbord of delight. Bug spray? Heck no. The occasional mosquito found in Arizona is swatted, not sprayed.

The most economical way to hunt is what is sometimes termed the "lets get a gang together and go get 'em." A camper fitted truck can carry a gang at about the same price charged for a single hunter. Dividing fuel costs can reduce that major expense dramatically. Four hunters, obviously, can make the trip at about a fourth of the cost of an individual. Turkey hunting bargains abound for the spring and fall hunter. The state of South Dakota is a good example.

The more than a million acres of public land within the Black Hills National Forest teems with turkey and other game. The streams and ponds of this great body of public land offer fine fishing for rainbow, western brook and brown trout. Public campgrounds offer facilities. Large campgrounds at Deerfield Lake, northwest of Hill City, Sheridan Lake, southwest of Rapid City, and Pactola Reservoir, due west of Rapid City offer accommodations to those who don't mind company. Smaller campgrounds abound.

A non-resident South Dakota turkey hunting license costs $40.00. Hunters who are also fishermen can purchase a 5 day fishing license for $14.00. Fall turkey hunters who develop a hankering to chase a deer with stick and string (South Dakota has both whitetails and mulies) can apply for one of the unlimited archery deer permits.

Splitting transportation costs three or four ways, tent camping or staying in a pickup camper or a travel trailer, a group of out of state hunters can enjoy a Merriams turkey hunt, plus fringe benefits, for about a hundred bucks each. A lot of welfare folks, in all probability, could afford that kind of hunt.

Out of state turkey hunts, properly planned, can be an exciting way to extend the season and can supply memories that will last a lifetime. Out of state hunts, quite simply, are one more advantage found in the great sport of spring and fall turkey hunting.

Some states offer combined deer and turkey hunts in the fall.

STATE BY STATE GUIDE

Alabama

Agency Name: Alabama Department of Conservation & Natural Resources, P.O. Box 933, Jackson, AL 36545; Ph 205-246-2165. Spring Season: Yes. Non-Residents: Yes. Reciprocal: Yes. Application Deadline: None. General Season Dates: Begins March 20, ends April 25. Above season dates are general, and vary by county. Decoys and electronic calls are not legal. Crossbows are not legal. Bag limit is 6 gobblers during spring and fall seasons combined.

Alaska

Spring Season: No. For more info: Alaska Dept. of Fish & Game, Subport Building, Juneau, AK 99801; Ph 907-465-4923. Arkansas

Arkansas

Agency Name: Arkansas Game & Fish Commission, #2 Natural Resources Dr., Little Rock, AR 72205; Ph 501-223-6359-6360. Spring Season: Yes. Non-Residents: Yes. Application Deadline: Not necessary or required. General Season Dates: Begins April 13, ends May 4, 1990. For a complete brochure on spring turkey season regulations contact: Information and Education Division, Arkansas Game & Fish Commission, #2 Natural Resources Dr., Little Rock, AR 72205 or phone 501-223-6300.

Arizona

Agency Name: Arizona Game & Fish Dept., 2222 W. Greenway Rd., Phoenix, AZ 85023; Ph 602-942-3000 ext 353. Spring Season: Yes. Non-Residents: Yes. Application Deadline: 1st Tuesday in January. General Season Dates: Begins last Friday in April, ends 3rd Sunday in May.

California

Agency Name: Fish and Game, 1416 9th Street, Sacramento, CA 95814; Ph 916-324-8930. Spring Season: Yes. Non-Residents: Yes. Application Deadline: None.   General Season Dates: Begins March 31, 1990, ends May 6, 1990. Virtually all private land hunting.

Colorado

Agency Name: Colorado Division of Wildlife, 317 W. Prospect, Fort Collins, CO 80521; Ph 303-484-2863. Spring Season: Yes. Non-Residents: Yes. Application Deadline: March 17, 1990. General Season Dates: Begins April 14, 1990, ends May 27, 1990. Hunter safety certificate required if born on or after January 1,

1949. Preference point given to unsuccessful applicants for limited permit areas. Most hunting opportunity occurs on private land; therefore, advisable to have permission before going hunting.

Connecticut

Agency Name: Connecticut Dept. of Environmental Protection, State Office Bldg., Hartford, CT 06115; Ph 203-642-7239. Spring Season: Yes. Non-Residents: Yes. Application Deadline: Permit hunting only, check with local or state DEP. General Season Dates: Begins May 2, ends May 22.

Delaware

Agency Name: Delaware Division of Fish & Wildlife, D. Street, Dover, DE 19901; Ph 302-736-4431. Spring Season: No.

Florida

Agency Name: Florida Game and Fresh Water Fish Commission, 620 South Meridian Street, Tallahassee, FL 32399-1600; Ph 904-488-3831. Spring Season: Yes. Non-Residents: Yes. Application Deadline: January 12. General Season Dates: Begins March 17, ends April 22. January 12 application period is for only 9 public wildlife management areas. There are 34 other WMA's open to spring turkey hunting that the application period does not apply.

Georgia

Agency Name: Georgia Dept. Natural Resources/Game & Fish Div./Game Management Section, 205 Butler St. S.E. Suite 1362, Atlanta, GA 30334. Spring Season: Yes. Non-Residents: Yes. Reciprocal: Only Florida honorary license holders. General Season Dates: Begins March 3, ends March 23.

Hawaii

Agency Name: Hawaii Division of Fish & Game, 1179 Punchbowl St., Honolulu, HI 96813; Ph 808-548-8850. Spring Season: Yes. Non- Residents: Yes. General Season Dates: Begins March 3, ends March 23.

Idaho

Agency Name: Idaho Fish & Game, Box 25, Boise, ID; Ph 208-334- 2920. Spring Season: Yes. Non-Residents: Yes. Application Deadline: March 2, 1990 for controlled hunts. General Season Dates: Begins April 9, ends May 6.

Illinois

Agency Name: Illinois Department of Conservation, Union Co. Refuge, Rt. 2, Box 628, Jonesboro, IL 62952; Ph 618-833-5175.

Spring Season: Yes. Non-Residents: Yes. Application Deadline: January 2-12, 1990 (initial drawing) after February 19 for remaining permits. General Season Dates: April 9-April 13, April 14-April 20 and April 21-May 2 (3 seasons). Non-residents should call permit office (217- 782-7305) for applications and permit fees information.

Indiana

Agency Name: Indiana Div. Fish & Wildlife, 607 State Office Bldg., Indianapolis, IN 46204; Ph 317-232-4082. Spring Season: Yes. Non- Residents: No. Application Deadline: Received by March 19, 1990. General Season Dates: Begins April 25, ends May 9.

Iowa

Agency Name: Iowa Department of Natural Resources, Wallace State Office Bldg., Des Moines, IA 50319; Ph 515-432-2823. Spring Season: Yes. Non-Residents: Yes. Application Deadline: January 8-February 2 (residents); February 8-March 2 (non-residents). General Season Dates: Begins April 9, ends May 6 (4 seasons: April 9-12, April 13-17, April 18-24, April 25-May 6). May not have non- resident season. If we do, hunters will need to write to the Iowa DNR for an application and return it between the February 8-March 2 period. Non-residents cannot hunt second season.

Kansas

Agency Name: Kansas Dept. of Wildlife & Parks, P.O. Box 1525, Emporia, KS 66801; Ph 316-342-0658. Spring Season: Yes. Non-Residents: Yes. Application Deadline: Units 1 & 2 January 26, Unit 3 May 6, Special Unit March 1. General Season Dates: Begins April 18, ends May 6.

Kentucky

Agency Name: Kentucky Dept. of Fish & Wildlife, Capitol Towers Plaza, Frankfort, KY 40601; Ph 502-365-7278. Spring Season: Yes. Non-Residents: Yes. General Season Dates: Begins April 11

Louisiana

Agency Name: Louisiana Dept. Wildlife & Fisheries, P.O. Box 278, Tioga, LA 71360; Ph 318-487-5885. Spring Season: Yes. General Season Dates: Begins March 17, ends April 29.

Maine

Agency Name: Department of Inland Fisheries and Wildlife, 284 State Street, Augusta, ME 04333; Ph 207-289-5252. Spring Season: Yes. Non-Residents: Yes. Application Deadline: February 1, 1990. General Season Dates: Begins May 8, ends May 28.

Maryland

Agency Name: Maryland Forest, Park & Wildlife Service, Natural Resources Bldg., Annapolis, MD 20401; Ph 301-974-3195. Spring Season: Yes. Non-Residents: Yes. General Season Dates: Begins April 18, ends May 16.

Massachusetts

Agency Name: Division of Fisheries and Wildlife, Field Hq., 1 Rabbit Hill Rd., Westborough, MA 01581; Ph 508-366-4470. Spring Season: Yes. Non-Residents: Yes. Application Deadline: March 25. General Season Dates: Begins May 7, ends May 26. Season is divided into 2 periods: May 7-12 and May 14-26. Hunter may select only one of these 2 periods. No Sunday hunting. Mandatory checking of birds within 24 hours of kill. No dogs, electronic calls, bait, live or artificial decoys. Permit application form attached to hunting license.

Michigan

Agency Name: Michigan Department of Natural Resources, P.O. Box 30028, Lansing, MI 48909; Ph 517-373-1263. Spring Season: Yes. Non-Residents: Yes. Application Deadline: February 1, 1990. General Season Dates: Begins April 23, ends May 27.

Minnesota

Agency Name: Department of Natural Resources, 500 Lafayette Rd., St. Paul, MN 55155-4007; Ph 612-296-3344. Spring Season: Yes. Non-Residents: No. Application Deadline: December 8, 1989 for Spring 1990. General Season Dates: Begins April 12, ends May.

Mississippi

Agency Name: Mississippi Dept. of Wildlife, P.O Box 451, Jackson, MS 39205; Ph 601-961-5300. Spring Season: Yes. Non-Residents: Yes. General Season Dates: Begins March 17, ends April 2, April 4, May 1.

Missouri

Agency Name: Missouri Department of Conservation, Box 180, Jefferson City, MO 65102-180; Ph 314-751-4115 Ex. #139. Spring Season: Yes. Non-Residents: Yes. General Season Dates: Begins April 23, ends May 6.

Montana

Agency Name: Montana Dept. Fish, Wildlife & Parks, 1420 E. 6th Ave., Helena, MT 59620; Ph 406-444-2612. Spring Season:

Yes. Non- Residents: Yes. Application Deadline: March 16 for areas with limited permits, otherwise no deadline. General Season Dates: Begins April 14, ends May 6.

Nebraska

Agency Name: Nebraska Game & Parks, 2200 N. 33rd St., Box 30370, Lincoln, NE 68503; Ph 402-471-0641. Spring Season: Yes. Non- Residents: Yes. Application Deadline: No deadline for unlimited areas. General Season Dates: Bow begins March 31, gun begins April 14, ends May 13.

Nevada

Agency Name: Nevada Dept. of Wildlife, P.O. Box 10678, Reno, NV 89520; Ph 702-688-1500. Spring Season: No. Nevada will consider a turkey season as early as spring 1991.

New Hampshire

Agency Name: Fish & Game Department, 2 Hazen Drive, Concord, NH 03301; Ph 603-271-1733. Spring Season: Yes. Non-Residents: Yes. Application Deadline: None, best time to apply is March/April. General Season Dates: Begins May 3, ends May 31.

New Jersey

Agency Name: New Jersey Division of Fish, Game and Wildlife, CN 400, Trenton, NJ 08625; Ph 609-984-6214. Spring Season: Yes. Non-Residents: Yes. Application Deadline: February 1-15, 1990. General Season Dates: Begins April 23, 1990, ends May 25, 1990.

New Mexico

Agency Name: New Mexico Natural Resources Dept., Villagra Bldg., Santa Fe, NM 87503; Ph 505-827-7835. Spring Season: Yes. Non-Residents: Yes. Application Deadline: February 15, 1990, Valle Vidal only. General Season Dates: Begins April 21, 1990, ends May 13, 1990.

New York

Agency Name: New York Bureau of Wildlife, Game Bird Unit, Wildlife Resources Center, Delmar, NY 12054; Ph 518-439-0725. Spring Season: Yes. Non-Residents: Yes. General Season Dates: Begins May 1, ends May 31.

North Carolina

Agency Name: North Carolina Wildlife Resources Commission, 512 N. Salisbury St., Raleigh, NC 27604-1118; Ph 919-733-7291. Spring Season: Yes. Non-Residents: Yes. General Season Dates: Begins 4/14/90, ends 5/12/90.

North Dakota

Agency Name: North Dakota State Game and Fish Dept., 100 North Bismark Expressway, Bismark, ND 58501-5095. Spring Season: Yes. Non-Residents: No. Application Deadline: February 21, 1990. General Season Dates: Begins April 21, 1990, ends May 13, 1990.

Ohio

Agency Name: Ohio Division of Wildlife, Foundation Square, Columbus, OH; Ph 614-265-6300. Spring Season: Yes. Non-Residents: Yes. Application Deadline: February 27 to March 13 only. General Season Dates: Begins April 23, ends May 12 - no Sundays.

Oklahoma

Agency Name: Oklahoma Dept. of Wildlife Conservation, P.O. Box 53465, Oklahoma City, OK 73105; Ph 405-521-3851. Spring Season: Yes. Non-Residents: Yes. General Season Dates: Begins March 31, ends May 6.

Oregon

Agency Name: Oregon Dept. of Fish and Wildlife, P.O. Box 59, Portland, OR 97207; Ph 503-229-5463. Spring Season: Yes. Non-Residents: Yes. Application Deadline: Tag sale deadline April 10, 1990. General Season Dates: Begins April 11, 1990, ends May 20, 1990. Hunter may take two turkeys during season provided two tags are purchased before tag sale deadline.

Pennsylvania

Agency Name: Pennsylvania Game Commission, 2001 Elmerton Ave., Harrisburg, PA 17110-9797; Ph 717-787-5529. Spring Season: Yes. Non-Residents: Yes. General Season Dates: Begins April 21, ends May 19.

Rhode Island

Agency Name: Rhode Island Division of Fish & Wildlife, 4808 Tower Hill Road, Wakefield, RI 02879; Ph 401-789-3094. Spring Season: Yes. Non-Residents: Yes. Application Deadline: Apply beginning March 1, no deadline. General Season Dates: Begins April 30, ends May 20.

South Carolina

Agency Name: South Carolina Wildlife & Marine Resources Dept., P.O. Drawer 190, Bonneau, SC 29431; Ph 803-825-3387. Spring Season: Yes. General Season Dates: Begins April 1, ends May 1. As a result of Hurricane Hugo, turkey hunting on the Francis Marion Hunt Unit will be difficult due to tremendous amount of fallen timber.

South Dakota

Agency Name: South Dakota Department of Game, Fish and Parks, 445 East Capitol, Pierre, SD 57501; Ph 605-773-3485. Spring Season: Yes. Non-Residents: Yes. Application Deadline: March 9. General Season Dates: Begins April 7, ends May 13.

Tennessee

Agency Name: Tennessee Wildlife Resources Agency, P.O. Box 4047, Nashville, TN 37204; Ph 615-781-6575. Spring Season: Yes. Non-Residents: Yes. General Season Dates: Begins March 31, 1990, ends May 7, 1990.

Texas

Agency Name: Texas Parks & Wildlife Dept., 4200 Smith School Rd., Austin, TX 78744; Ph 512-389-4774. Spring Season: Yes. General Season Dates: Begins April 17, ends May 6 (Eastern Turkey East Texas April 7-22).

Utah

Agency Name: Utah Division of Wildlife Resources, 1596 W. North Temple, Salt Lake City, UT 84116; Ph 533-9333. Spring Season: Yes. Non-Residents: Yes. General Season Dates: Begins May 1, 1990, ends May 20, 1990.

Vermont

Agency Name: Vermont Fish and Wildlife Department, 103 S. Main St., Waterbury, VT 05676; Ph 802-244-7331. Spring Season: Yes. Application Deadline: No deadlines, need to purchase turkey tags $5.00. General Season Dates: Begins May 1, ends May 31.

Virginia

Agency Name: Virginia Dept. of Game & Inland Fisheries, 4010 West Broad St., Richmond, VA 23230-1104. Spring Season: Yes. General Season Dates: Begins April 14, ends May 19, 1990.

Washington

Agency Name: Washington Dept. of Wildlife, 600 N. Capitol Way, Olympia, WA 98504; Ph 206-753-5733. Spring Season: Yes. Non-Residents: Yes. General Season Dates: Begins April 18, ends May 13 (tentative dates to be set January 19 at Commission meeting).

West Virginia

Agency Name: West Virginia DNR - Wildlife Resources Division, State Capitol Complex, Building 3, Charleston, WV 25305; Ph 304-348-2771 ext 17. Spring Season: Yes. Non-Residents: Yes. General Season Dates: Begins April 23, ends May 19.

Wisconsin

Agency Name: Wisconsin Department of Natural Resources, Box 7921, Madison, WI 53707; Ph 608-266-8840. Spring Season: Yes. Non- Residents: Maybe, after all resident applicants receive permits. Application Deadline: For Spring 1990, the application deadline was November 3, 1989. General Season Dates: Begins Wednesday, April 11, 1990, ends Sunday, May 20, 1990.

Wyoming

Agency Name: Game and Fish Department, 5400 Bishop Blvd., Cheyenne, WY 82009; Ph 307-777-6974. Spring Season: Yes. Non-Residents: Yes. Application Deadline: February 1- March 1, except Black Hills is general - license may be bought from the Cheyenne office until the end of the season. General Season Dates: Begins 1st Saturday in April, ends 1st Sunday in May.

TURKEY CALLS
CHAPTER FOURTEEN

Learning to talk fluent turkey is a task that might take a lifetime. Maybe more than that. Some folks, sad to say, work all of their lives on the accent and the cadence and never get a decent handle on it. The wild turkey, fortunately, does not demand perfection. Most will settle for less and some will settle for a lot less. A hen turkey known to the author may have been the sorriest turkey talker in Coconino County (Arizona). The speech impediment did not seem to make her less attractive to the toms. She had the usual complement of suitors. Later, about fall, she was seen parading with an impressive gang of healthy poults.

This Kelly Kallers Whistle Box duplicates the fall call of a young turkey.

Some tom turkeys can find it just as difficult to talk fluent turkey. There is a time in the life of every jake when his pitiful gobble causes the older guys to wrap their wings around their sponge and rudely guffaw. Sort of a cross between a coyote yodel and a soprano with the croup.

Some of those jakes fight the speech problem for all of their lives. Turkey may be a bit like humans in that aspect. Some are able to talk in well enunciated and melodious tones that would make a politician envious. Others are more Elmer Fuddish. That wide range of style in turkey talk is a benefit to hunters who go afield and make an effort to talk turkey. The turkeys, much of the time, will loudly applaud even the most basic effort.

Modern turkey calls can be loosely classified into two broad categories. Calls that produce a sound because of friction and calls that produce a sound because of air. The friction calls, almost always, are easier to use than the air activated calls. The well known and reliable box call is a good example. This rectangle of wood, usually cedar or walnut, has one or two sharp edges on the sounding board. The lid, or paddle, is somewhat curved. The chalked surfaces are stroked to provide right good yelps and clucks. With practice the box can be used to produce a decent sounding purr and even a gobble.

The box call has two obvious strengths. A raw novice can practice on the box a bit and produce decent yelps, clucks and purrs. The nature of the construction causes those calls to be loud and long distance. Many very good turkey hunters take their toms with a box call year after year.

The Lynch Turkey Call Company has been making box calls for more than 50 years. President Allen Jenkins has owned the company for about half that time.

As is the case with any instrument a box call must be treated with some respect if it is to remain in tune. Water can warp the wood causing a change of tone. Too much moisture in the air can do the same, but to a lesser degree. Dirt, grease or grime on the friction surfaces can also affect tone. With reasonable care a box call should last a lifetime and maybe more. Many box calls have been passed down to several generations of turkey hunters.

The slate call, actually a slate and a peg, is another ancient and reliable instrument that works because of friction. The sound is produced by pushing a fire hardened wooden peg, or a peg made of some other material, across a smoothed section of slate. Many modern slates come from the maker with both a wood and a Plexiglas peg. Pegs come in varying lengths and with a variety of handles, each producing a slightly different tone. The Plexiglas peg has an advantage over the wooden peg. Once the slate is wetted the wooden peg slides instead of biting and no sound is produced. A Plexiglas peg works wet or dry.

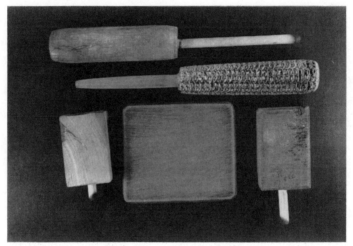

Each of these pegs produces a slightly different tone.

Some "slate" calls have the slate replaced with another material. Rough finished glass is a common substitute. A decent slate type call can be made by using a slab of the naturally occurring glass called obsidian.

The slate (or glass) call can produce purrs that will cause a gobbler to immediately fall in love from an acre away. Quality clucks are also easy to produce on a slate or glass call. Slates can be used to produce decent yelps.

The friction that causes the slate type calls to sound is a bit like the friction that causes a blackboard to squeak when a fingernail is drawn across it. The sound produced, fortunately, is a lot less aggravating to both human and turkey ears.

Like the box, the slate demands care if it is to be kept in top form. Grease or oil on the slate, the glass, or the peg will cause trouble. The slate surface will become work worn and must be renewed. This is easily accomplished. Use a medium grit sandpaper to scour away contaminants and to remove the marks left by peg use. To keep the surface of the slate completely flat, tape the sandpaper, rough side up, to a sheet of window pane glass. Turn the call so that the slate comes into contact with the sandpaper and scour until the surface is cleaned.

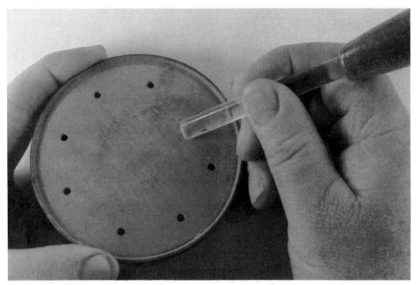

Unlike the wood peg, the Plexiglas peg works wet or dry.

Each slate will have a "sweet spot", an area that delivers the best tone. Walking the peg around the slate will usually allow discovery. Mark the wood edge of the call by cutting a small notch at the sweet spot. You will be able to find that sweet spot by feel, even in the dark of a pre-dawn set-up. With a bit of practice, actually a very little bit, nearly anyone can use the slate and peg to produce purrs, clucks and yelps.

Most of the other friction calls are a variation of the box or the slate. The "Push Button Box" is a small wooden box without a lid. A spring tensioned push rod extends through the box to cause two chalked surfaces to drag when the rod is pushed. Most such calls are tuned to produce a hen yelp. Others may be tuned to produce other turkey sounds. One on the market does a decent job of producing one of the fall calls, the so-called kee kee run lost call of the young turkey.

Air activated calls, much of the time are a bit more difficult to master than the friction calls. Some hunters, extremely talented callers, go to the woods and use their vocal cords to produce many or all of the sounds made by a wild turkey. Hunters who have tried this, those who kept at it until they got good and those who kept at it but still stayed bad, say it is a difficult skill to master.

A sucking smack causes the wingbone call to articulate authentic yelps.

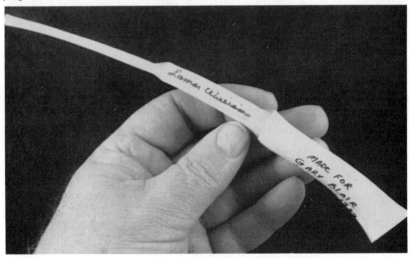

This three bone wingbone takes practice but delivers deadly yelps.

An air call that has been around almost as long as there have been turkey hunters is the wingbone call. This old and faithful instrument is made by gluing turkey wingbones together, usually from a hen turkey killed in the fall, to form a long and hollow tube. Sucking one end of the call produces excellent yelps. The bad news is, the wingbone call is a bit difficult to master. Those who work with the wingbone long enough to conquer it, however, seldom use any other call.

The diaphragm call, in one of its many configurations, is the air activated call that is most often used by turkey hunters. One or more thin reeds of latex are stretched around a metal (usually aluminum) horseshoe shaped frame and secured to the frame with duct tape. The call is fitted to the roof of the mouth with the open end of the horseshoe facing forward. Exhaling air from the chest (or the diaphragm) causes the reed to vibrate. Multiple reeded diaphragms, as a general rule, have the potential to produce a greater diversity of sounds. Some manufacturers notch the reed (split reed calls) or reeds to add to the tone and complexity of calls possible.

A diaphragm call of the proper type can be used to produce authentic sounding yelps, putts, clucks, purrs, cackles, whistles and kee kees. A man (or a woman) who has mastered the diaphragm call can even gobble.

Cupping the hand controls tone and volume of diaphragm call (R).
The call is slipped in the mouth with open end of horseshoe facing out.

The diaphragm call has a number of obvious strengths. The diaphragms are easy to make and market, which causes the price to be low. The hunter is able to talk turkey without moving the hands, a decided plus when the bird is in close giving that suspicious lump at the base of the tree the bad eye. Using the mouth call permits the hands to grasp the gun at the ready, cutting down somewhat the reaction time when it becomes necessary to outdraw a gobbler.

Like all other calls, maybe more so, the diaphragm call must be cared for if it is to last longer than a hunt or two. Latex, sad to say, begins to deteriorate the day it is made. Saliva can increase the rate of deterioration. To get maximum life out of a diaphragm call keep it out of the sun. After each hunt wash the call in warm water containing a bit of liquid detergent and rinse. This removes most of the material that causes the condition scientifically known as slobber rot. Place the wide end of a flat toothpick between the rubbers if it is a multiple reeded call to keep them from welding together as they dry. Finally, when not in use, keep the calls refrigerated in a clean container (an empty and cleaned oleo tub works well) to prolong life.

Another type of air activated call is the latex covered tube sometimes called the snuff box call. Stretching one of the latex reeds across half of the mouth of an empty 35 MM film canister and securing it with a rubber band produces a decent call of this sort. This call is also made and marketed with the latex stretched across a part of a wooden tube. In any configuration snuff box type calls can be used to produce a great long distance yelp. Many callers use the snuffs as a locator call, knowing that this little call has the power needed to reach out and touch the gobbler that roosts off near the county line.

Multiple reeds, split reeds, or notched reeded diaphragm calls causes the tone to become lower pitched and more raspy.

131

The thin latex reed, exposed as it is to brush and other hazards, is easily torn. Experienced callers carry a spare rubber or two in their emergency repair kit.

In a pinch some commonly available items can be substituted for a formal call. Many a turkey has lost his life because a hunter held a blade of grass or a section of a leaf to his lips to make a seductive hen call. Other emergency calls can be made from other material. One caller used the bottom of his ball point pen as a makeshift wingbone call and fetched in a longbeard. Another once used a small section of toilet tissue (unused) to call a tom.

At times spring toms can be called using a call that imitates the sound of a gobble. Experienced hunters who work hard hunted woods use this call with caution. Hiding out in the brush to make a call that sounds like an illegal turkey can be dangerous. Making a call that sounds like a legal turkey is asking for double trouble.

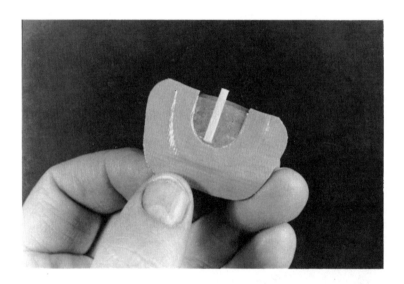

Slipping a section of a flat toothpick between the reeds hastens drying and lengthens call life.

The most effective gobble call is a rubber tube that looks to be a six inch section of thin walled hose. A diaphragm reed within the hose is vibrated as the hose is shaken vigorously and a downright good gobble is produced. Turkeys that absolutely refuse to take one step toward the best made hen yelp have been known to come at a dead run to the gobble. There can be times when the gobble call is used with a diaphragm yelper to make the target tom think some strange hunk is messing around with one of his girls. Jealousy, it seems, can sometimes be a stronger motivator than lust.

Getting a tom to gobble can sometimes be a chore. Experienced hunters use a variety of techniques to get those tight mouthed toms to sound off. The most common of these locator calls is the hooter. Such calls make an authentic imitation of the barred owl's "who cooks for you" and can be used to decently imitate the hoot of the great horned owl. The hooter is most effective at dawn and at dusk.

The crow call can also be used to locate a spring gobbler. Crow calls usually consist of a plastic reed fitted between two hard plastic bite rods and with the entire assembly fitted into a wooden tube. The crow call is easy to use and does a good job of imitating the raucous cry of the crow. Unlike the owl call, which works best close to dawn and dusk, the crow call can be used up into the day.

Some hunters, looking for locator calls that the turkey is not sick of, have turned to unconventional sounds. Some use a call that produces the honk of a Greater Canada with success. Others use a predator call that simulates the distress cry of a prey animal, usually a cottontail or blacktailed jackrabbit. Coyote howls and elk bugles have been used with some success.

The hooter call carries less volume than a natural voice hoot but is simple to operate.

The Red Wolfe Gobble Call delivers an authentic sounding gobble when it is shaken.

133

The turkey call used, it should be noted, is less important than the caller. A moderately talented hunter can take about any call and talk fluent turkey. They can cluck and they can yelp. They can kee kee and cackle. That's what practice does. In the following chapters well known turkey takers, all skilled callers, will share the technique they use to take the toughest tom. With their advice, and with practice, any dedicated hunter will do as well.

Snuff box type yelpers are loud and help to locate far away turkey.

USING THE BOX CALL
CHAPTER FIFTEEN

A famous turkey hunter, at one time or another, probably said something like: "The surest way to call a turkey is to go to good turkey habitat, find a comfortable place to sit, and stroke sparingly on a box call from first light to last light." If a famous turkey hunter did not say that he should have. Turkeys, being both curious and gregarious, will eventually creep in to check out the action. The author relearned that truth while on a tough spring hunt for Merriams.

It was not a great year to be hunting turkey on the Navajo Indian Reservation. Hot dry winds coupled with unusually high temperatures had caused the turkeys to turn shut mouth. The toms would gobble a time or two from the roost but would develop lock jaw when they hit the ground. It may have been too hot for thoughts of love. The birds would graze a bit, eat a grasshopper if he came close, and would then shade up.

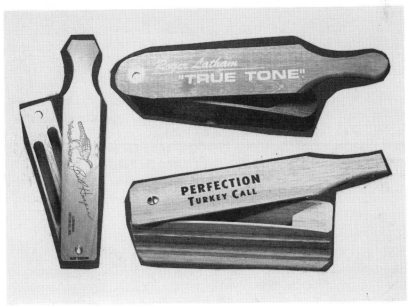

Box calls come in a variety of configurations and price ranges. Each will call turkey if properly used.

It was mid-afternoon, the hottest time of the day, and shading up sounded to be a good idea. The author and his companion found a comfortable set up (in the shade) close to an area that showed gobbler activity. Strut marks decorated the pine needles, and in other areas close by, evidence of foraging was present. The most difficult part of the set up was managing to stay awake long enough to scrape out three or four plaintive yelps every ten minutes or so.

Two hours passed with no action. Companion was sound asleep and the author was nearly so. Unexpectedly, from a hundred yards out, came one weak and barely interested gobble. Three soft yelps and a putt later a paranoid two year old tiptoed to twenty yards. The shot put the turkey to sleep and awakened companion. That turkey was taken and tagged because the author merged two deadly techniques, patience and the deadly sound of a well stroked box.

Box calls are semi-simple in design and are semi-simple to operate. They are, essentially, a hollow rectangle of wood that has the top edges of the two long sides finished to a sharp lip. A wood paddle is screwed to one of the short ends of the rectangle top. Scraping the chalked paddle across one of the lips creates friction and causes a sound. The resonance built into the box causes the sound to imitate the yelp, the cutt, the cluck, and the purr. The paddle can be snugged to the lips with a rubber band and shook to produce an acceptable gobbler.

Turkey hunting history tells us that the Gibson Box was the first box call marketed. This venerable box call (old heirloom Gibsons are still in use and are much in demand as collector's items) was made from a solid piece of wood that had been hollowed out.

M. L. Lynch, a pharmacist, began building box calls as a hobby. Mr. Lynch was a retired military man and was an avid turkey hunter. His first efforts duplicated the Gibson box but he found it difficult to control the tone. He experimented until he designed a call made of wood pieces glued together that delivered a constant and predictable tone. In 1940, realizing there was a demand for the calls, he began marketing the Lynch Box and it is marketed to this day.

Mr. Lynch travelled through turkey calling country to market his calls through local sporting goods stores, or if none was available, through hardware stores. Many times he would set up a sidewalk stand to sell his calls directly to the consumer. Raking out melodious yelps on one of the box calls nearly always attracted a crowd in record time.

Allen Jenkins, the current owner, joined the company in the late 1960's and attained ownership a few months later. A lifetime of hunting the wild turkey, and a lifetime of box call manufacturing, has caused Allen Jenkins to be a respected authority. The Lynch box, Allen says, duplicates the yelp of a hen turkey more closely than either a mouth call or a slate call. The Lynch Box, Allen states, is the deadliest tool available to the turkey hunter.

Floridian Doyle Loadholtz, a talented natural voice caller, sometimes boxes to rest his vocal cords.

Boxes make the best sounds with the least amount of practice. Common sense care causes the box to last the lifetime of the purchaser. Many Lynch calls have been willed from father to son to start a second or third generation of use.

Every box call made, and there are many box call manufacturers at present, has a "sweet spot", a place where the tone is a bit more rich. Many of the manufacturers, Lynch is one, fine tunes each call before it leaves the factory so that the call is sold sounding as good as it can sound. Other manufacturers sometimes market a call that is less perfectly tuned. Hunters can fine tune the call by carefully changing the tension provided by the hinge screw. The paddle should hit the lip at the same point each time it is stroked. That contact should be at or near the middle of the paddle.

The inside of the paddle, the curved part, must be chalked before use. The type of chalk used can affect the tone of the call. Some chalks, the so called "dustless" chalks, are made dustless by adding a wax to the formula. The wax tends to decrease the fiction and dilutes the sound. Use waxless chalk, the kind sometimes sold as carpenters chalk.

Even a box that has been properly chalked with the correct kind of chalk will glaze at the point of contact after repeated use. The "bite" can be restored to the wood by carefully scuffing it with 220 grit sandpaper. Scuff, do not sand. The goal is to remove the glazed chalk without changing the curve of the paddle.

As is the case with all musical instruments common sense care is important. Bill Moss, who makes and markets the Moss Double Tone Box, suggests keeping the box in an old bread wrapper (author turns his inside out to remove the small worry about bread grease) when calling during a rain. Water, Bill says, can permanently damage a box.

Store the box in a warm dry place when not in use. The dashboard of your vehicle is not an appropriate place. Sun rays, multiplied by the windshield glass, can cause warpage and a permanent loss of tone.

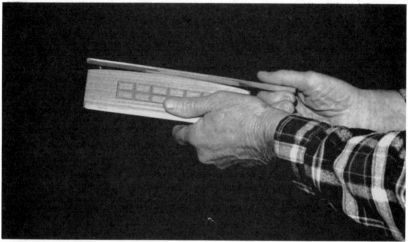

Neil Cost demonstrates correct hand position for making the yelp.

Correct hand position for making the cluck.

Yelps, clucks and purrs are easily made on a well tuned box call. Rest the bottom of the box in your left hand (if you are right handed) and tilt the box to the right. Grasp the paddle between thumb and forefinger of the right hand and move the paddle to the right. Avoiding downward pressure, stroke the paddle back to the left so that the curve of the paddle scrapes across the lip. Repeat several times, developing a measured cadence of yelps.

Neil Cost (The Gobbler) P.O. Box 1444, Greenwood, South Carolina, is a custom call maker who traces the origin of at least one of his designs back to the Gibson Box. That call, for those interested in history, was patented by H.C. Henry Gibson on January 5, 1987. The call was made from a solid block of white walnut (butternut). Mr. Gibson called the device a Turkey Caller and Gobbler on the patent application.

Neil makes a call that is somewhat similar to the Gibson call. Cost's Old Missouri Boat Paddle call is of somewhat like design. Why the name? A hunter who has this oversize call, according to Cost, can remove the lid, climb into the trough of the body, and use the lid to paddle across any river he may come upon during the hunt. The call, even though it is larger than the "standard" box, is not all that big.

The call that Neil Cost made for the author is constructed of white walnut body and straight grain red cedar lid. The tone must be heard to be appreciated. It may produce the most authentic hen yelps of any call available.

A well made and well tuned box call, Neil feels, can be a tyro turkey hunter's best friend. Even old time turkey hunters, those who sleep with a diaphragm or two resting between cheek and gum, almost always carry a box as a back up when they get serious about turkey hunting.

The box sound most often used to take a wild turkey, according to Neil, is the lost call. The yelp. "More turkeys gave been killed using a yelping box," he says, "than with all of the other calls combined."

The most important element in turkey hunting, according to Cost is woodsmanship. Too many hunters, he feels, do not take the time needed to acquaint themselves with the land they plan to hunt and with the habits of the turkeys. A second important reason for failure is not leaning to use your call proficiently. Knowing what to say, and when to say it, can be crucial. Many of those who are new to the sport of turkey hunting, Neil feels, call too long and call too loudly. Neil says this even though he admits he himself calls long and loud when he talks turkey. The difference is experience. Neil has stroked a box so often it is nearly an extension of his voice.

Hunters new to the sport do not have that degree of calling skill and should reduce volume and calling frequency.

Another cause of failure is stroking out the wrong kind of yelps on the box. Many hunters, Neil Cost claims, take too long a stroke. The yelp that is produced is more like a jake yelp than a hen yelp. A boss tom will gobble until he develops laryngitis but will seldom respond.

Many hunters, Neil says, do not respond correctly when they elicit a gobble. "Some new hunters hear a gobble a half mile off and immediately turn timid," he says. They sit down right there and call soft and seldom, expecting that far away gobbler to come at a dead run. Most of the time he won't do that. It is usually necessary, according to Neil, to move on that gobbler to get into a setup that makes it easy for him to respond.

Neil has advice on other aspects of turkey hunting. "Turkeys can't count," he claims, "and do not know that a lot of hunters think they are supposed to yelp only two or three times then shut up." Cost sends out short choppy hen yelps and may produce 15 or 20 yelps in a string. Volume will be varied depending on circumstances. If the gobbler is distant, or if he is trying to locate a gobbler, Neil calls loudly. If the gobbler is close, call volume is reduced.

Camo carrying case for the box call is a needed accessory.

A hunter who goes to the woods to talk to the turkeys before season opens, in Neil's opinion, should be arrested and held in solitary until turkey season ends. Such "sport" educates the turkeys and makes them more difficult to call when season starts.

M.L. Ashley (310 S. 10th Avenue, Lanett, AL 36863) is a second custom call maker who draws inspiration from the Gibson box.

Ashley's Big Box is exactly that. Big. If it is proper to call Cost's call a Boat Paddle it would likely be as correct to call Ashley's Big Box a two man canoe. This handsome friction call is a fraction of an inch less than one foot along the base of the body and is one foot exactly along the lid. Like the Gibson, Ashley's Big box is worked from a single piece of red cedar. The call made for the author strokes out a fine raspy hen yelp, quality clucks and perfect purrs.

Box calls and box call variations abound. The Moss double tone mentioned earlier (P.O. Box 1112, Sedalia, MO 65301) comes equipped with a double lip on the right edge of the body. The second sounding board adds a deep toned resonance seldom found in conventional boxes. The Moss Double Tone Box Call comes in the company of a cassette instruction tape.

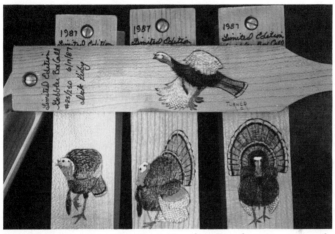

Some collector series, like these Quaker Boy boxes, are works of art.

All of the box calls are functional. Some makers add beauty and collectability. The Limited Edition Box Calls made and marketed by Quaker Boy in 1987 is a good example. The lid top of this four set series is decorated with an oil painting (each call is hand painted) of a gobbler strutting, walking and flying. The calls came in numbered sets of 250 and each was signed by Quaker Boy President Dick Kirby.

Every call maker, and every caller, has his or her own way of playing the box. Here are tips from Master Turkey Talker Neil Cost that explains his technique of talking turkey.

To make the yelp, hold the bottom of the base loosely in the left hand with the thumb up on the left side. Offset the top to the right. Hold the top down very lightly against the lip and move it across the lip in a straight across motion. Do not be tempted to make the lid bind or lift off the lip. Make a series of cadenced short strokes to produce a string of yelps.

To CACKLE do just as you would for the yelp but make the top strike rather than cross smoothly over the lip. This can be done by exerting a very slight downward then upward motion of the top without pause. Start slowly then pick up the tempo, then let it fade at the end. About 10-12 of these made in the right tempo will produce a fine cackle.

To make a CLUCK hold the call loosely with the left palm as you did for the yelp. Offset the top to the right until the left side of the lid is about half of the way across the trough. Hold down the left side of the lid with the thumb of the left hand only enough to keep it from rising as you tap the right side back toward the left with your right hand. If you allow the palm of your right hand to push against the handle very slowly a PURR will be produced.

The tone of the cluck can be controlled by varying the amount of offset. As a general rule, the farther to the right the higher the pitch. A series of high pitched soft clucks made very fast will produce a CUTT. A fair CACKLE can also be made in this manner but can better be made as a part of the yelping sound.

The LOST CALL of the young hen or gobbler is made by making the same type of strokes as you would for the yelp except make them as long as possible. Make about 8 or 10 of these long regular spaced strokes and make them as loud as possible. After a couple of series strike the opposite lip of the box sharply a couple of times then let the lid drag across the lip to produce a WHINE or a PURR. Do not be afraid of a mistake. Call loud. When you receive a response keep clucking and yelping to make the young bird keep coming. This call will bring up the young hen as well as the young gobblers, so be sure of your target before you shoot.

To make the GOBBLE place a #10 or #12 rubber band around the call about an inch in from the handle end of the body. Turn the box away from you to grasp it on the bottom end with handle up. Shake hard four or five times. A natural gobble will result.

Here are tips that will keep your box call working well. Keep the box dry. If it gets wet dry it out slowly, maybe atop your television set. Do not sand the underside of the lip unless rechalking does not correct defects in sound. NEVER sand the lip of the call. A white non-oil based chalk is best. Blue carpenters chalk is next best. Never use "dustless" chalk and do not wax or polish your box call.

The Roger Latham "True Tone" box call marketed by Penn's Woods Products (19 West Pittsburgh Street, Delmont, PA 15626) is a box that is somewhat similar to the old Gibson design. The body of the call is a solid piece of wood routed to provide a trough. The lid is made of the same material. Both body and lid are heavy duty. The look of the box delivers a testimonial attesting durability.

The author received an insight into the durability of the True Tone while on a turkey hunt in Kansas during the 1990 season.

The author and a local hunter were out before dawn to hunt a piece of private land. The turkeys had moved to roost on an adjoining tract of land, a place that was off limits to the hunters. The two parcels of private land were separated by a 160 acre field of ankle high wheat. The two hunters set up as near the property line as possible. The local pulled out a venerable Roger Latham True Tone box and stroked out a series of deep toned yelps. The gobblers roosted across the field boomed out their appreciation. "They are interested," the local whispered confidently. The author, accustomed to working sophisticated turkeys, nodded agreeably but remained secretly skeptical. The local raked out another short series on the well used (even abused) Penn's Woods product and the gobblers answered right back. "They are coming," the local confided. The author remained skeptical. A second or so later three black dots became visible at the far field edge and each of those dots were racing for the property fence a bit like O.J. Simpson charging the goal line. Less than a minute later the three turkeys, all jakes, crossed to the hunter's side of the fence and stood ten feet away from the guns, looking desperately for the hen.

Frank Piper, president of Penn's Woods Products, markets the popular Roger Latham box call.
Photo from Frank Piper's files.

The Roger Latham box brought jakes and longbeards at a hard run.

Later that same day the hunters, who had eschewed the jakes, were working a hardwood ridge on another property and the scarred box brought in three longbeards, birds that came not quite as enthusiastically as the teenagers, (they could not as they ran the

143

danger of tripping on their beards) but who came at a trot. The local admitted later he had owned the call for seven years and customarily carried it on the dash of his hunting and work truck.

Roger Latham, for those few who do not already know, was at one time the director of research for the Pennsylvania Game Commission and is nationally recognized as a leading expert on the wild turkey.

Box calls have a lot going for them. They are easy to use and are versatile. Boxes are handsome and durable. And they are moderately priced. Considering all of that it is not surprising that the box call has stayed immensely popular with turkey hunters of all skill levels since that day nearly a hundred years ago when Henry Gibson patented his design on the Gibson box.

Two hours of work on the box put the gobbler to sleep and awakened the hunter. (Photo by Lovett Williams.)

144

USING THE DIAPHRAGM CALL
CHAPTER SIXTEEN

The diaphragm turkey call, sometimes simply named the mouth call, is the most versatile turkey call available. In the right mouth the diaphragm can be convinced to articulate yelps of all types, cutts, clucks, cackles, purrs and even gobbles. The simplicity of design causes the mouth call to be one of the best bargains in calls currently available. Unlike all of the other call types, the diaphragm can be sounded without using the hands. No hand use means no hand movement that might cause a crazy in love tom turkey to rethink his commitment. Are you ready for the bad news? The diaphragm, in all of its configurations, is the most difficult call to master. Some expert diaphragm callers insist that a hunter must swallow one diaphragm of every color before he or she gains proficiency.

Walk-ins like this Black Hills hunter can carry a selection of the compact and lightweight diaphragms.
Photo: Mark Kayser, S. Dakota Dept. of Tourism.

Even though that statement is an obvious exaggeration, becoming proficient with a diaphragm call takes practice and dedication. But thousands of new hunters take their turkey each spring using the diaphragm as a caller. A Flagstaff, Arizona hunter, out in the pines making his first try for a spring Merriams, was one such.

Perry Shirley is an Arizona Highway Patrolman who is a hard hunter. He had not previously hunted spring turkey, however, until he got lucky in the lottery held shortly after New Years Day. Knowing he had a lot to learn between the draw and the opening day of the season (about two months) Shirley got serious about learning calling skills. He purchased a pair of double reed diaphragm calls and an instruction tape. And he begged, borrowed and rented every article and every video that dealt with the sport of spring turkey hunting.

Perry practiced calling between stops out on the highway. He played the cassette tape to learn how the yelps, clucks and cackles should sound and practiced until he was at least able to slobber out a fair duplication of the yelp. On opening morning he made a tough hike up a dead dark wilderness ridge to match wits with the bird he had been told was the smartest, most sharp eyed critter in the woods.

Cupping the hand can cause the call to be more directional.

Shirley gained the ridgetop too late to find the birds on the roost. He wandered the woods yelping occasionally and yelped up a gobble in short order. The tyro turkey hunter set up with his back against a 200 year old yellow bark ponderosa and sent out a few frugal yelps. A hot gobble answered right back. A few minutes later three monstrous Merriams strutted to 30 yards. A fourth was on the way when Perry ended the hunt. The bird carried a beard that was a scant half inch short of a full foot. The 22 pound bird (big for a Merriams) won Perry first place in a local big turkey contest, providing a quart of Wild Turkey whiskey and a fistful of money.

Many competition callers use the diaphragm call as their main contest call. Two time world champion Eddie Salter of Evergreen, Alabama is one. Using calls of his own manufacture Eddie is able to reproduce nearly every call the wild turkey makes.

Hunters starting out on the diaphragm, in Eddie's opinion, should begin with a single reeded call taped taut to a lightweight small frame. Such a call fits most mouths better and the single reed of thin latex is easier to control than some of the more sophisticated multiple reed or split reed diaphragms.

The call should be placed in the mouth with the open end of the "horseshoe" facing forward. Move the call so far forward in the mouth that the ends bump the eyeteeth. Ease the tongue up to touch the latex and exhale air between the tongue and the latex. Do not be concerned about the quality of sound produced. The goal at this point, according to Eddie, is to make any kind of sound.

The first sound produced will likely be a high pitched keee. Mouth kee-youk as you continue to blow. Practice will let you refine the sounds.

Champion turkey callers Tom Duvall and Jim Clay of Perfection Turkey Calls (Box 164, Opequon Ridge SHB, Stephenson, VA 22656) have marketed an excellent video tape on the basics of calling. The tyro caller is told and shown basics such as diaphragm placement, air control, changing the tone using mouth control, and the kinds of calls to use to produce different kinds of turkey talk. Here is good advice taken from that tape.

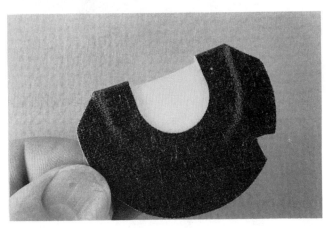

Cutting a notch in the edge of the tape can aid in positioning during a pre-dawn set-up.

A single reeded call is high pitched. Adding membranes, or reeds, deepens the pitch. Splitting the reeds causes the call to become raspy. Perfection calls are color coded to indicate type of construction.

Color, obviously, is not an aid in the dead dark of a pre dawn setup. Duvall suggests cutting a notch in the skirt at the right side of the call so that it can be placed in the mouth properly (with short reed down against tongue) by feel.

If the skirt of the frame is too large for a comfortable fit in the mouth, use scissors to slightly trim the skirt until it fits.

Wet both sides of the latex reed and place the call in the mouth with the open end of the horseshoe facing forward. Clay advises a position about midway between the soft palate at the back of the mouth and the teeth. Bring air up out of chest in short bursts (those who have played a wind activated musical instrument will have an easier time learning breath control). Say CHUCK or CHIRP as you expel chest air between the latex reed and your tongue. Practice until you are able to duplicate the yelp and the cluck. These may be the only calls you will need to call and kill a turkey. Learning other calls, however, provides more weapons to use when needed.

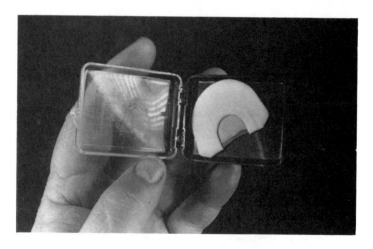

Protect the diaphragm from dirt and from sunlight.

Clay likes to call fast and choppy in the spring. The tone of the call can be changed by opening or closing the mouth to different degrees, or by varying tongue pressure.

Diaphragm calls do not tolerate direct sunshine. Leave one on the dashboard of your vehicle for an hour or so on a warm day and the call is likely ruined. Keep the diaphragms in a container in the refrigerator during the off season to extend the life of the call.

Learning to master the diaphragm call is mainly a matter of determination. Purchase one or two single reeded calls, one or two multiple reeded calls, and a split reed or two. Purchase the Clay-Duval instruction video and perhaps an instruction cassette or two marketed by one of the competition class callers. Seriously consider buying the series of cassette tapes (marketed by Real Turkeys, 2201 S.E. 41st Avenue, Gainesville FL 32601) that contain the actual calls of the wild turkey. Use all of those tools to practice, practice, practice. Before you know it your wife will be packing for a visit to mother, the dogs will run for the shed each time you put something horseshoe shaped in your mouth, and you will be able to yelp, cluck, cutt and cackle decently. All of that, when it comes right down to it, is a small price to pay for proficiency.

This amateur turkey talker used a diaphragm call to call in this monster Merriams.

150

USING THE SLATE
CHAPTER SEVENTEEN

The slate call, sometimes called the peg and slate, is as equally old as the wingbone call and the box call. Like the box call, the slate call makes a sound as a forced friction contact is made between two surfaces, between the thin slice of slate and the peg. The main strengths of the slate are simplicity, reliability and versatility. The main defects are a lack of volume, failure to work in wet weather, and the fact it takes two hands to work the peg and slate property.

The slate is basically a three part call. The thin slab of slate, sanded smooth, is one. The sounding board that holds the slate is another. And the peg, in a variety of configurations, is the third.

A few minutes of practice with a peg and slate has the tyro turkey talker producing decent yelps, clucks and purrs.

The sounding chamber is most often made of wood, usually walnut. Sounding chambers can be made of a variety of other materials. The author has in his call collection a slate caller made for him by the noted turkey biologist and writer C.H. Kit Shaffer of Lynchburg, Virginia. That call has the slate mounted on the shell of the common box turtle. An important purpose of the sounding board is to prevent the hands from coming into contact with the slate itself, thus dulling the sound. The hollow space produced by the sounding chamber adds to the tone of the call also.

The peg can also be made of a variety of material. Hardwood dowelling, fire hardened at the point and with a corncob fitted at the opposite end, is the most common. Pegs can have other material as holders and can be made of material other than wood. A plastic Lucite rod has become recently popular. And although the Lucite has not the tone delivered by the wood peg, the tone is certainly acceptable to both the caller and the callee. The Lucite peg has at least one advantage over the wood peg. If the wood, or the slate, is wetted the friction between peg and slate is destroyed and the call will not sound. The Lucite peg will work on the slate equally well wet or dry.

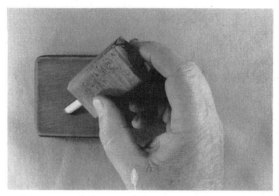

Changing the size and shape of the peg can cause a tone shift.

Some call manufacturers have modified their friction call line to include a glass call. The glass call is nothing more than a slate call where the slate is replaced with a roughened sheet of glass. Glass friction calls can be worked with wood or Lucite pegs, just as the slate calls are.

Glass calls like this double Cutter Glass from Kelly Kallers work well wet or dry.

Nearly all hunters, with a minimum amount of practice, can yelp, cluck and purr on a slate well enough to call a turkey.

Changing the peg material, changing the length of the peg, even changing the angle of contact between the peg and the slate can cause a change in tone. Experienced callers carry a variety of pegs to use as conditions dictate. Some are able to create subtle changes in tone by altering their hold on the peg. Grasping the peg tightly, in most instances, can cause the tone of the call to imitate the high pitched voice of a young turkey and of some hens. Holding the peg loosely deepens the tone to imitate the voice of a raspy hen or a male turkey.

The surface of the slate must have enough "bite" to grab the peg point. Grease or oil on the slate will kill the bite. The hunter must use sandpaper, or some other scouring agent, to restore the bite to the call. It is important that both the slate surface and the peg be protected from contaminants. The small amount of oil present on the human skin, many times, will cause the slate to go mute, or at the very least, undergo an unpleasant change in tone. Camo paint, the kind used on hands and face in lieu of gloves or a facenet, can pose a deadly danger to a slate call.

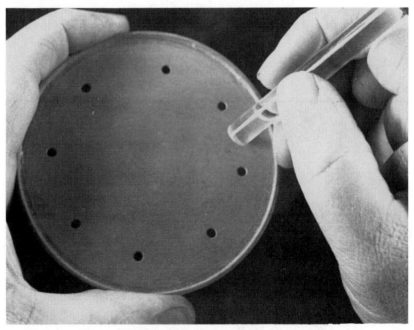

Push the tilted peg from slate edge toward your body.

Every hunter has his or her own "best" way of working the slate and peg call. Right handed hunters generally make a half circle of the thumb and forefinger of the left hand to hold the base of the sounding chamber. The middle finger of the left hand rests on the sounding chamber bottom as added support. The hand holding the sounding chamber and the slate can be braced against the stomach (or against a drawn up leg if sitting) to provide more stability.

The peg (sometimes called the striker) is held between the thumb and forefinger of the right hand, braced by the middle finger, in much the way that a pencil is held for writing. Place the peg on the most distant part of the slate, angle the peg at about a 60 degree angle away from you, and push the point of the peg across the slate to you. Varying the amount of pressure put on the peg will control volume and somewhat vary tone.

To make the yelp, cause the point of the peg to travel a small circle around one part of the slate. The point of the peg is never lifted from the slate as this small circle (about 1/2" diameter) is repeated.

To make a cluck place the point of the peg on the slate, angle the handle away from you, and snap the peg point forward and up.

To purr with the slate call place the point of the peg on the slate near the far edge, angle the handle away from you, and push the peg across the slate for about a half inch. Pull the peg back, maintaining contact between peg point and slate (no sound will be produced) and repeat.

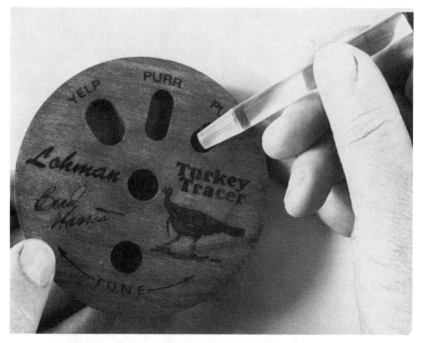

The Lohman Turkey Tracer simplifies slate call use.

A variation of the purr is the harsh and loud purr voiced by a pair of fighting gobblers. The author saw Bill Harper use this "challenge purr" to call in a paranoid longbeard while on a south Texas hunt. To make the challenge purr on the slate, push down hard on the angled peg to increase friction. Push as you would for the purr and a challenge purr will result. Slow the push so that a series of fast clucks are produced and you are cutting.

Most slate and peg calls are similarly constructed, although the slate and the sounding chamber may vary in shape and in material. Some are made round to better fit the hand. Others are free formed and some are rectangular. In each of the configurations the slate surface will have a "sweet spot" that sounds the best to your ears (and perhaps even to a turkey's ears). Find that spot and mark it by cutting a small notch in the rim of the wood or plastic at that point. You will now be able to locate the sweet spot by feel, even in the dead dark of a predawn setup.

Hard hunter Bill Harper sometimes calls with a diaphragm to locate a turkey and uses a peg and slate to call him close.

At least one turkey call company offers a somewhat simplified slate call. The Turkey Tracer marketed by Lohman Manufacturing is a round of slate fitted into a walnut frame. A second piece of walnut covers the top. The top has oval cut-outs that control peg movement, facilitating the production of yelps, putts and purrs. The walnut top can be rotated so that each owner can tune his call to suit his or her ear.

Few hunters will live long enough to wear out a well made slate call, even if they use it every day of every season for all of their life.

Keeping the slate working well takes a minimum of effort. Preventing grease or oil to contaminate the slate surface is the major concern to clean the surface.

The drag of the peg across the slate can produce wear marks and the slate surface must be renewed by scouring at occasional intervals.

If the slate is framed in wood (most are) protect the wood from warpage by keeping it dry. If the wood is unavoidably wetted, dry it slowly. Place the call on the top of the television or near some other low heat source until it has dried.

Keep the wood away from prolonged exposure to the hot sun. The dashboard of your truck is a poor place for a slate call. The sun's rays, magnified by the windshield glass, can cause warpage of the wood. Warpage of the wood can cause the slate to be stressed and that can cause the slate to crack.

In the right hands, coupled with woodsmanship, the peg and slate caller can be a deadly instrument for the taking of turkey. Every serious turkey hunter should add at least one, and a selection of pegs, to his collection of calls.

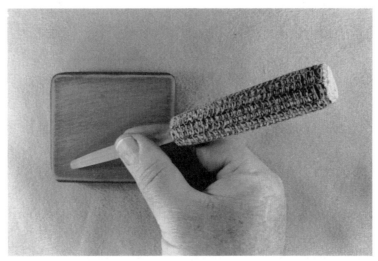

Move peg to different areas of the slate to locate "sweet spot".

EASTERN TURKEY TACTICS
CHAPTER EIGHTEEN

The Eastern turkey, in the view of many experienced turkey hunters, can be the hardest turkey to hunt. Is the Eastern inherently smarter than his poor old dumb western cousins? Probably not. Hunting pressure, according to Alabama hunter (and two time world champion turkey caller) Eddie Salter, causes a dumb Eastern to get dead fast. Those that survive the first few days of the season smarten up. Give that same turkey an entire season to evaluate the hunting style of the dozens of hunters who challenge him and you are looking at one tough turkey. The hunter who ties his tag to an Eastern longbeard is either a very good hunter or a very lucky hunter. Maybe both.

Calling proficiency, Eddie says, is not often the most important ingredient in a successful turkey hunt. And even though that statement may seem to be strange, coming from a man who won the world championship of turkey calling in 1985 and 1989, and missed it by one point in 1990, other world class callers agree. Woodsmanship, most say, can be the most important element in the taking of a turkey.

World Champion caller Eddie Salter thinks Alabama turkey become burnt out on some kinds of calls.

"Turkeys are not like turkey calling judges," Eddie Salter observes, "and do not expect perfection in calling. Knowing the habits of the turkey, knowing every feature of the land you are to hunt, can be the difference between success and failure. The Eastern turkey is usually a hard hunted turkey and is no pushover. Try him out with a few calls, maybe plain yelps, to learn if he likes your calling. If he does not, back off and call sparingly. If the turkey responds enthusiastically to your calling, however, give him lots of it, get really aggressive. I usually let the turkey tell me the technique that will bring him close."

Knowing the location of streams can let the hunter modify the setup to avoid hang-ups.

Knowing the lay of the land, through pre season scouting or through information provided by topographic maps, can be a critical element in success. "There are a lot of streams in Eastern turkey habitat," Eddie Salter observes, "and any one of them, in the wrong place, can cause an Eastern bird to hang up. Knowing the location of those streams, of fences, and other obstacles lets the hunter avoid them when he or she makes the setup." Eddie relearned this lesson while on a 1990 spring hunt with an outdoor writer. He had called the bird to about sixty yards but the out of sight bird hung up and refused to come one step more. Eddie spent a lot of time talking turkey to that bird, world class calling. The bird gobbled enthusiastically at everything Eddie said but was all talk and no walk. Finally Eddie and the writer made a half circle to go to the bird. A small stream, they discovered, had caused the hangup. A couple of understated yelps at the new setup brought the tough bird at a run.

Eddie Salter does all of his competition calling with a diaphragm. He uses the diaphragm on his turkey hunts but also carries other calls. "I have given a bird my best series of yelps, cutts and cackles on a diaphragm call," he admits ruefully, "and been ignored. Changing to a slate can cause that same bird to come running." Hard hunted birds, Eddie feels, can become burnt out on a certain kind of call. Changing to present a different kind of turkey talker can cause these jaded birds to regain their interest. Eddie Salter normally carries three kinds of calls on his hunts. He carries a box call and uses the box mainly as a locator call, because of the built in potential for volume. He carries diaphragms of his own manufacture and does most of his calling with one of those. He carries a slate and peg call to add a bit of diversity to his turkey talk.

Mississippi hunter Preston Pittman, another world champion caller, agrees that it takes more than excellent calling to make a turkey hunter. Using his natural voice the 16 year old Pittman won the prestigious Mississippi State Calling Championship, beating out some of the best turkey callers in that calling state. "I could make nearly every call that the wild turkey makes using my voice," Preston recalls, "but did not have the expertise it takes to be a good turkey hunter." This came but it took time.

Being a competition class caller has helped Preston to make more than a few tough turkeys. While on a hunt with outdoor writer Tony Kinton he encountered a gobbling bird that was hung up across a high banked creek. Preston decided to do a series of calls he often demonstrates at his turkey calling seminars, a flock of birds watching a fight between a pair of gobblers. Using a variety of calls Pittman produced the drumming and gobbling of the toms, the coarse but immature yelps of a jake, and the excited clucks of the hens. It wasn't long until turkeys began to fly across the creek to them, more than a dozen in all. The hunt ended successfully because of Preston's calling ability.

Hunters who are less skilled at calling, Preston feels, hunters who may be visiting the turkey woods for the first time, often make a basic mistake. They become enthused at the variety of turkey calls on the market and buy one of each. And they take that collection of calls to the woods and try to do too much with them. It would be better, this good caller and good hunter feels, to stick with one kind of call. Work with that one call, maybe a box or a slate, maybe even one of the simple to use push rod box calls, until the hunter is confident with that kind of call. Take that call out on the hunt and use it sparingly. Even some very good callers have a tendency to overcall in the woods, he feels, and a hunter who is new to turkey hunting has that tendency also. It is better, Preston feels, to call sparingly. "A beginning hunter who attains a fair degree of skill on the call and who is a good woodsman can take tough turkeys here in the part of the south I call Dixie (Georgia, Mississippi and Alabama)," Preston concludes. "And the most important aspect of the hunt is woodsmanship, knowing the habits of the wild turkey and knowing every wrinkle of the land you intend to hunt."

Missouri hunter Brad Harris knows Easterns and feels that set-up can be critical to success.

Brad Harris is a man who hunts for pleasure and sometimes hunts for a living. Brad is public relations director for Lohman Game Calls, a Missouri based game call company. Brad is in the woods a lot each spring, hunting with and guiding company clients and friends. The author was on a spring hunt with Harris during 1990 and had the opportunity to see this hard hunter in action.

A hunter who sets up on a turkey, Brad feels, should be considerate. That hunter should make it easy for the turkey to come to the set up. And to do that, the hunter must know the lay of the land and make the setup to avoid natural barriers.

Even though he has called turkeys from far away ridges, Brad feels the hunter should set up as close to a roosted turkey as it is safe to do, using stealth and skill to make the approach unobserved. The "eighteen wheeler tom" Brad called to the author's gun was a good example.

The birds were roosted in a hardwood grove that grew next to a paved county road. A green field of foot high wheat was on the far side of the grove and a very cold and very wet waist high stream split the grove. Brad led the sneak, moving only when an eighteen wheeler (about the only traffic that time of the morning) rumbled by. Ten minutes, four eighteen wheelers and three creek crossings later, Brad motioned to make the setup. A few minutes later the gobbler flew down, and as expected, lit in the center of the wheat field. Several soft yelps later a bobbing white head could be seen above the young wheat. Calling played a very small part of that kill. The main element of success was picking a setup that was close to the roosted bird, making the sneak without being discovered, and picking a setup that made it easy for the bird to respond to the call.

Hard hunted birds can develop an amazing amount of call resistance. Toms who have collected a harem of hens can be a particularly hard sell. Here are two tricks that might cause a tom with hens to be more cooperative.

Proper setup can make it easy for the tom to come close for the shot.

The first technique requires almost no action on the part of the hunter. Many times a gobbler who is a hard sell at dawn can turn into a sex maniac before noon. Yelp a few times to the gobbler to let him know there is a lonesome hen about and then let him leave with his harem. By midmorning most, maybe all, of those hens may sneak off to lay. There is a good chance the gobbler will come tiptoeing back to investigate the lonesome hen yelp he heard at daylight. A bit of calling, much of the time, can bring that tom in at a run.

Setting up close to a roosted tom, Brad Harris feels, makes it easy for the tom to come to the call.

The second technique that can be used to take a tom with hens is a modification of a very successful fall technique. If the gobbler will not come because he has hens, get rid of the hens. Scatter that flock of birds and use lost hen yelps to call the gobbler to the gun. The flock can be scattered from the roost the night before, at dawn, or if the lay of the land permits, after they hit the ground.

Silence can be a deadly tactic to use on a hard hunted Eastern tom, or on any other tom. Hunters often encounter birds who come enthusiastically and vocally to about fifty or sixty yards and then hang up. These birds will gobble at every call but will not come one step closer. A hunter needs to decide why the bird has hung up. If the hunter knows the lay of the land and guesses there is an obstruction that has caused the hang up, it is proper to move on that bird to call from a setup that has no such deterrent. If the hunter knows there is no logical reason for the hang up it is reasonable to believe the bird has stopped because of paranoia. The best course of action, in many instances, is to do nothing. Shut up and let the bird worry about the love he nearly had but has lost because of timidity. Many times a few minutes of silence can cause the bird to sneak in for a look. Much of the time that sneak will be made silently.

A modification of the technique where the sound of silence is used against the bird is the "I'm insulted and I am getting the hell

Silence can be a deadly technique to use on a tough tom.

out of here" technique. Best done with two hunters on the set up, one hunter sneaks away from the bird calling forlornly as he goes. The gunner stays put. Much of the time the hard sell tom will follow the departing hen yelps, bringing him to gun range.

If you are alone on the setup, make the bird believe you are leaving. Turn your head away from the bird if you are using a mouth call, cup one hand over the mouth to further muffle the call, and yelp softly.

Quaker Boy president Dick Kirby sometimes uses a different technique to unhang a hung up tom. He gobbles. "I don't like to use the gobble," Dick cautions, "as it can be dangerous to your health." But the gobble, he says, can be an effective call. Dick had worked a tough Pennsylvania tom that resisted the world class caller's best efforts. The gobbler was vocal but not athletic. He would answer nearly every call but would not lift one foot. Finally the tom had Dick so hot he was willing to try about anything. He gobbled out a lusty challenge. The tom answered right back. Dick and the tom exchanged insults a time or two more and Dick shut up. Five minutes later the tom was spitting from eighteen yards out and Dick spit back with a smoothbore. Being patient and being willing to try something different let Dick tie his tag to the leg of this really good three year old.

A bunch of hunters will work most Eastern toms during the course of a season. Like any other hard hunted turkey the birds become call resistant. The hunter who scores consistently will be the hunter who hunts hardest, who is the best woodsman, and the one who is not afraid to try new techniques.

163

HUNTING THE OSCEOLA
CHAPTER NINETEEN

The Florida turkey, the turkey commonly called the Osceola, occupies the most restrictive range of any of the sub-species of the wild turkey. The bird some folks call the swamp turkey hangs out in the swamps and lowlands of south Florida, specifically the peninsula of Florida. When all is said and done geography determines identification. A bird that lives in the area designated as Osceola habitat is an Osceola, even though he or she may exhibit physical characteristics of the Eastern subspecies.

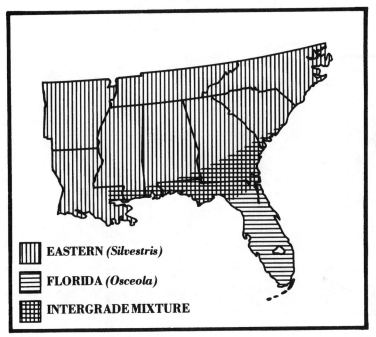

EASTERN *(Silvestris)*

FLORIDA *(Osceola)*

INTERGRADE MIXTURE

The peninsula of Florida has been designated as Osceola range. (Sketch courtesy of Lovett Williams).

The restricted range, and the preponderance of private land within that restricted range, can cause the Osceola to be a tough turkey to take. Resident and non-resident hunters generally have two options when it comes time to hunt the Osceola, private land hunts or public land hunts. Public hunting areas are managed by the Florida Game and Fresh Water Fish Commission. Seasons and permit numbers are set on a year to year basis. The number of permits issued for these public areas are limited to avoid overhunting. The permits are offered on a first come first served basis. Hunters who do not apply promptly are often disappointed. Deadlines can come early. In 1990, as an example, January 12th was the deadline to apply for nine of the 43 WMA's. To obtain current information on turkey hunting on the wildlife management areas contact Florida Game and Freshwater Fish Commission, 620 South Meridian Street, Tallahassee, FL 32399-1600 (904-488-3831).

A guided private land hunt is the best bet for hunters who hanker to hunt the Osceola. Photo by Lovett Williams.

Hunting opportunities exist on many tracts of private land. The best option for those who are unfamiliar with the area and unfamiliar with the Florida turkey likely lies with one of the outfitter guide services. The State of Florida does not require guides or outfitters to be licensed so no list is available. Lovett Williams (2201 S.E. 41st Avenue, Gainesville, FL 32601) is a good contact. Another is

Jim Conley's Outdoor Adventures, 606 Pinar Drive, Orlando FL 32825). To locate other outfitters/guides check the classified advertisements that appear periodically in *The Turkey Hunter* and in *Turkey Call.* Or call one of the five regional offices, or the Tallahassee Office, of the Florida Game and Freshwater Fish Commission. Ask to speak to someone who has knowledge of turkey hunting opportunities. Much of the time some person in the office will have personal knowledge of local guides.

Even though the Florida turkey is sometimes called a "swamp turkey", there is no good reason to do so according to Lovett Williams. Some of the Osceola habitat is swampy, true enough, and the turkeys there have modified their behavior in response. The Florida turkeys who live on the dry flatlands, however, behave about the same as any other flatland turkey behaves.

Bobcat abound throughout Osceola habitat and sometimes respond to turkey talk. (Credit U.S. Forest Service).

The turkeys that occupy the watery habitat will wade the water if it is not above their knees (about six inches) according to Williams.

This can confuse hunters who are unfamiliar with the swamp turkey's habits. Some may set up with shallow water to their back, assuming that the water will limit a rear approach. Much of the time they assume wrongly and the gobbler will come sloshing in to the call.

Osceola hunters may have other surprises. The state of Florida, according to Lovett Williams, has lots and lots of bobcat. So many, in fact, that they are considered to be the number one predator of adult turkeys. More than a few hunters have been amazed to see one of the spotted felines creeping in on the setup. A time or two the hungry bobcat has leaped onto the hunter, resulting in a very surprised hunter and a very surprised bobcat.

Lovett Williams has spent most of his life as a wildlife biologist studying the wild turkey, the language of the wild turkey, and the habits of the wild turkey. Here are tips provided by Lovett that might help a hunter who is after an Osceola turkey, or any of the other sub-species of the wild turkey.

Dr. Williams has identified 31 separate sounds in the wild turkey language. As biologists learn to better recognize the subtle nuances of the turkey language there will likely be more. A very few of those identified turkey sounds are helpful to hunters. The most useful, in Lovett's opinion, is the plain yelp during the spring season and the kee kee run during the fall season. The lost yelp is an effective call during both spring and fall seasons. Turkeys are social birds and may respond to the yelping simply because they have an interest in getting together with others of their kind.

Many turkeys have been taken using unsophisticated calls like the push rod yelper.

Hunters who have a limited amount of experience in the turkey woods should not be overly concerned with the articulation of "perfect" turkey calls. Turkeys do not demand perfection from other turkeys and they do not often demand perfection from the hunter. Many turkeys have been called and killed using the simple push rod friction call.

Lovett feels that novice turkey hunters should do a lot of calling while in the turkey woods. The more practice a hunter gets, he says, the better his calling will be and the more confidence he or she will have. And although some might respond just as well to less sophisticated calling, there is no penalty attached to being better than you have to be. Some turkeys, those who have had a recent bad experience with a turkey talking hunter, might respond to "expert" calling when they would not respond to calls that sounded less like a turkey.

There can be times when overcalling will be counterproductive. Too much calling to a roosted gobbler can cause him to become excited and can cause him to gobble repeatedly. As long as the dialogue continues the gobbler may stay on the roost, expecting the hen to come close so that he can see her. That excess of gobbling may attract other hunters.

It has often been said that convincing a gobbler to come to a hen yelp causes him to "go against nature's way." Lovett Williams believes that this is basically a true statement. When the breeding season is in full swing, when many gobblers have collected hens, nature has programmed receptive hens to go to the gobbles. Nature, however, does not rely on a single strategy to assure reproduction. There will be times when the gobbler goes to the hen and there will be times when both gobbler and hen travel toward each other.

"I think a gobbler is more apt to go to a hen early in the season," Williams says, "because the hen is not coming to the gobbler." If the turkeys are going to get together the gobbler must do the travelling. Biologists know that the toms have a tendency to follow the hens around because turkeys like to be with other turkeys. The toms may go to the hens simply because he is interested in other turkeys, not necessarily because one gives a love call that says "come on over here boy..I'm hot to trot." That gobbler might come just as quickly to a gobbler yelp as he does to a hen yelp.

Can a turkey tell the sex of another turkey simply by hearing that turkey's voice? Lovett thinks so but is not sure. He recalls setting up to call turkey to the camera late in the breeding season. Hen decoys were positioned but the toms paid little attention to them. When Lovett yelped like a gobbler he got little response. When he yelped like a hen the gobbler's heads would turn white, and if they were not too far along into turning into summer turkeys, would strut.

169

Lance Vincent used a Lynch Box Call to summon the world record Osceola (the bird is also the overall champion). Allen Jenkins, president of Lynch is in background.

There is a variation in turkey voices just as there is in human voices. Young turkeys imprint on the voice of their mother and know that voice from the voice of all other hens. Some hen turkeys, in all likelihood, have somewhat deep voices that are more gobbler like. Some gobblers, likely, have a voice that is high pitched, somewhat hen-like.

Although no studies have documented the phenomena, it is likely that turkeys have dialectal differences in somewhat the same way humans have regional accents such as the southern drawl and the Yankee twang. Dialectal differences have been noted in some species of birds, particularly those birds who are very vocal. It is reasonable to assume that turkeys, very vocal birds, speak in dialects.

An effective early spring call, one that is seldom used, is the fighting pert. Early in the breeding season, when the bachelor bands of gobblers are breaking up, fights between gobblers are somewhat frequent. It is in a turkey's interest to know who is dominant in the neighborhood and other turkeys will sometimes come rushing in from all around when they hear the fighting rattle. This call is easily made with a slate call. Place the point of the peg on the side of the slate (or glass) that is most distant from the body, tilt the peg at an angle, and push the point of the peg to you. Apply a lot of pressure to the peg so that friction is increased. A loud aggressive purr can be produced, and if the pressure is sufficiently severe, a series of loud and aggressive clucks.

The diaphragm is a versatile call but lacks many of the esthetics of more permanent types.

Some turkeys can identify the voice of individual turkeys. These poults have imprinted on their mother's voice and can select it from all others. (Rhodes photo.)

The type of caller used, according to Lovett Williams, is a matter of personal preference. Lovett prefers to use the wingbone caller (although he stipulates that it is sometimes difficult to master) or his natural voice. Beginning callers, he feels, might find the diaphragm call the most versatile call on the market. Versatile but not perfect. The diaphragm, in Lovett's opinion, is not durable, not pretty, made of synthetic material, and does not have the appeal of a wingbone, the slate or the box call. There is something about all of those, in Lovett's eyes, that provokes a sense of permanence. Each is an instrument that can be cherished for all of a turkey hunting lifetime, an instrument that can accumulate memories of contests lost and won. Each is an instrument that can be bequeathed to the next generation of turkey hunters.

Dr. Lovett Williams has authored a number of books dealing with the wild turkey. His "The Art and Science of Wild Turkey Hunting", "The Book of the Wild Turkey", and "The Voice and Vocabulary of the Wild Turkey" are recommended without reservation.

Even though the Florida turkey is sometimes called the "swamp turkey" many spend their entire lives on dry land.

172

HUNTING THE RIO GRANDE TURKEY
CHAPTER TWENTY

Turkeys of the Rio Grande brand hang out in the wild wild West, the somewhat wild West, and in a few spots where even a wild look in the eye can cause problems. The main habitat of the bird is in the state of Texas. It is not an exaggeration to state that about 500,000 of the long legged Rios call the Lone Star state their home. Rio Grande turkeys can also be found in Oklahoma, in Kansas, within a very restricted habitat of eastern New Mexico and a few other places. The Rio has been introduced to California, Hawaii and other far west habitats but interbreeding with other races have somewhat diluted the race.

There are more than 500,000 Rio Grande turkeys in Texas, and that is no tall tale.

The name *Meleagris gallopavo intermedia* reflects the namer's opinion that this turkey is intermediate in appearance (and range). Sort of Eastern appearing in one aspect and Merriams looking in another. The Rio is a bird that has adapted well to a diversity of habitat, none of it prime turkey country in the conventional concept. Rio Grande turkeys in south Texas prosper on the grasslands of vast cattle lands. The grasslands are interrupted somewhat frequently by groves of mesquite and oaks, areas that provide food, cover and roost sites. As is the case with the Merriams turkey of the far west, the Rios of south Texas find that stock ponds provide a steady and dependable source of water.

173

Rio Grande habitat in other parts of Texas, in Oklahoma, Kansas and New Mexico can be considerably different. The mesquite is still present in areas, but the land is wetter. In some areas year round streams nourish large cottonwoods that serve as roost sites. In other areas groves of large cottonwoods border agricultural areas to provide habitat necessities.

Much of the Rio Grande range is on private property. Statistically speaking, perhaps 98% of the range is in private ownership. Those who own the land have learned to manage turkey and other wildlife on their land just as they would any other resource. They see the turkey as a cash crop and manage it accordingly. Some of the ranches will permit hunter access for a small fee. Others offer full service hunting operations, providing guides, meals and lodging. Some even offer airport pick up and drop off. As services increase so does the charge.

Feeders congregate Texas turkeys in sanctuaries set aside for photographers and wildlife watchers.

Some of the Texas hunting operations, it should be mentioned, go the extra mile to insure hunter success. Light activated corn feeders are triggered shortly after dawn and at dusk. Deer, turkey and other game are attracted. Shooting stands, erected close to the feeders, provide comfort and concealment for the shooters.

A second common technique also uses corn as a bait. A pickup truck pulls a corn spreader over ranch roads a day or two before season. It doesn't take the turkeys long to discover this bounty and they gather around the roads to feast. On opening day, and thereafter, shooters are transported along the roads. When they see a turkey they jump from the vehicle and shoot him before he can run out of range. At times, hunters will walk off into the woods, following the turkeys, set up, and make an attempt to call them close. Such attempts are seldom successful.

Ranchers who run these bait and shoot operations (legal in the state of Texas) do so because a percentage of their guests pay their money to kill a turkey and wish to do so with the least expenditure of effort. Those same ranches will not force any hunter to road blast a turkey if it goes against his nature. Those hunters, the ones who opt for a higher quality hunting experience, are free to pursue the turkey using the technique that suits their skills and their conscience.

Other Texas hunting operations run a more traditional type of turkey hunting operation. Hunting guests are supplied with a guide who knows at least the basics of turkey calling. A gobbler is roosted at dark and the guide and hunter move in before daylight the next morning to work that turkey.

The author hunted Texas turkey during the 1989 spring season and learned several interesting facts about hunting south Texas Rio Grandes on that particular ranch.

The hunt took place on the half million acre Kennedy ranch headquartered near the south Texas town of Sarita. The accommodations were grand. Guests were housed in comfortable motel-like rooms located on the grounds. Maid service was provided.

An indication of turkey numbers came at dawn the next morning, a couple of days before season opened. Dozens of gobbles, perhaps hundreds, competed for attention. Before long, turkeys of all size and sex came flying, running, creeping and crawling into the ranch compound to receive their share of bounty from the dawn triggering of the corn spreader (no hunting or shooting was allowed within the square mile surrounding the ranch buildings). White tailed deer, some still carrying antlers, came with the turkeys. The ranch yard was a wildlife photographers paradise.

On opening day of turkey season the author travelled the ranch roads, accompanied by a ranch employee, before dawn, hunting up a gobble. Such was easy to find. The gobblers that hung around near the ranch roads, however, were hard sells. They would gobble a time or two at locator calls, or at a yelp, but would then turn shutmouth. Most refused to come one step toward the caller.

Those road turkeys, it seems, had learned to distrust any turkey talk that came from the direction of the road, or talk that was preceded by the sound of a vehicle engine.

Bill Harper, a legendary turkey hunter from Neosho, Missouri, showed me a couple of tricks that turned the hard sell turkeys into romantics. The first thing we did was to leave the vehicle and proceed on foot.

Walking through the oak mottes Bill would pause every hundred yards or so to yelp using a Lohman #836 double reed diaphragm turkey call. Within one half hour we heard a distant gobble. Moving fast, we closed on that turkey and made the setup when we were probably within one hundred yards. The turkey remained interested and was obviously moving to the setup. At exactly the wrong time, a pair of hunters walked between us and the bird and that setup was ended.

Two tracks (locally called senderos) cut through oak mottes to provide access to prime turkey territory.

One hour later, two miles down the road, we repeated. This time the turkey came to about one hundred yards and hung up. We were in the middle of a very thick oak motte and visibility was limited, as was shooting opportunity. Bill Harper switched to a new, just out of the package Lohman slate and used it aggressively. The purrs and clucks produced sounded nothing like the satisfied purrs and querulous clucks often heard from a hen. These were gobbler clucks and gobbler purrs, sounds often heard at the scene of a no holds barred gobbler fight. The hung gobbler unhung and moved our way. Cautiously. One slow step at a time. Eyes alert to discover the least danger.

Shooting lanes were short because of the oaks. The gobbler sneaked in to about fifteen yards before a clear shot was offered. One shot from the borrowed stack barrel Weatherby made the clean kill. The bird was big by Rio Grande standards. Twenty-two pounds and with the long sharp spurs (1½") that is typical of the Rios.

My second bird (Texas has a two bird limit) was a pound bigger. Both birds carried impressive ten inch beards.

Although there are small tracts of public land that house Rio Grande turkeys in both Texas and Oklahoma, the competition for the turkey on those lands can be awesome. Some require interested hunters to submit applications and permits are issued as a result of a lottery. Rio Grande turkey hunting is essentially a private land hunt.

How does a hunter go about locating a ranch that permits access or an outfitter that supplies guided hunts? The classified advertisements found in both the *Turkey Hunter* and *Turkey Call* list both ranches and outfitters. Those issues published just prior to the spring season usually carry the most listings. Try a letter to Texas Parks and & Wildlife to learn if they can recommend an outfitter who does business in your area of interest. Use some of the same techniques mentioned in Out of State Hunts (Chapter 13).

Some Texas ranches offer spring turkey hunts that can be combined with a hunt for javelina (pictured) or a great variety of imported wildlife.

Spring and fall turkey hunters who travel to Texas can collect an uncommon dividend. Many of the ranches have introduced exotic game from other countries. The Nilgai, (or bluebuck) is an elk sized antelope imported from India. African antelope such as the Blackbuck are also available. Feral hogs and the hoglike javelina are permissible targets as are mouflon sheep. The prices are surprisingly modest.

The fall turkey season coincides with the whitetail deer season in Texas. The license bought for turkey also allows the harvest of up to five deer (some must be doe).

Fall turkey hunters can take advantage of the generous Texas whitetail season.

Texas offers one further advantage to the hunter who is handy with a camera. Many of the ranches maintain no hunting areas where turkey and deer are attracted by baiting. Many have photography stands that offer an excellent opportunity for photography. Take along the longest lens you have, and if that lens is larger than about 200 MM, take along a tripod.

The Rio Grande turkey hunting in Texas is about as good as turkey hunting gets. And that is no Texas tall tale.

Hunting the Rio Grande turkey in Kansas can be equally rewarding. Kansas stocked Rios beginning in 1965 (the birds came from Oklahoma flocks) into the southwest and south central part of the state. The birds prospered. Good hunting can be found in a number of wildlife areas classified as public lands. Places like Fall River, Kaw, Kingman and Cimarron National Grasslands. As is the case in Texas, much of the Rio Grande habitat is on private land.

The State of Kansas recently enacted legislation that allows non-resident hunters to hunt turkey. The Kansas flock is estimated to be in excess of 100,000 and the big birds are found in 105 Kansas counties. Success rate averages about fifty percent.

The eastern third of Oklahoma is Rio range. The spring limit is set yearly and can vary from county to county. The most generous permits the taking of three turkeys. Like Texas and Kansas the main part of the Rio range is on private land, land that is leased to individuals and hunting clubs on a yearly basis. Non-resident hunting is allowed.

The Rio Grande turkeys who get their mail at a Kansas or Oklahoma zip code, almost always, are fatsos when compared to the lean and trim Texas Rios. A more generous habitat accounts for the obesity. The 22 pound Rio the author took in Texas would hardly cause comment in either Kansas or Oklahoma.

The State of Kansas offers an excellent opportunity to hunt heavyweight Rios.

HUNTING THE MERRIAMS
CHAPTER TWENTY-ONE

The Merriam's turkey is mainly a bird of the ponderosa pine forests of the west. Islands of habitat dot some southwestern states like Arizona, New Mexico and Nevada. Restocking efforts have extended the Merriams range east, north and west of the historic range. The magnificent Merriam's (named to honor the zoologist C. Hart Merriam) can currently be found, and in most cases hunted, from Nebraska west to Washington State and from Arizona north to the Canadian border. Recent restocking efforts in Canada have established a nucleus population there.

The Merriams turkey is migratory through much of his range. (Photo by Bob Miles, Arizona Game & Fish Dept.).

The Merriam's (Meleagris gallopavo merriami) is migratory through much of it's range. The flocks follow the receding snow line in early spring to move high up on the mountains to graze on the succulent green spring grass, to work the insects brought out by the warming weather, and to breed. The short migration is reversed in the fall as winter white blankets the high country. The Merriams move back to the lower limit of the ponderosa pine belt and even on down into the foothills that house transition woodlands.

181

The limiting factor for many of the western turkey is water. It is a strange truth that western areas that receive more than a hundred inches of snowfall in a winter can be water starved in July. The turkeys need the water more in July, when it is scarce, than they do in December when warm winter days can cause a snowmelt that fills the normally dry waterways.

The lack of available water can cause a particularly acute problem through the turkeys southwestern range. Turkey flocks there, for the most part, hang out in one of the several vast acreage of National Forest land. That land is public domain that has been designated multiple use land and is almost always covered with cattle during the spring and summer months. Ranchers have constructed earth dams along the drainages (locally called mud tanks or stock ponds) to conserve run off from snowmelt and the sometimes torrential summer rains. Those stock ponds provide water for the turkeys and other wildlife.

Trick tanks (guzzlers) provide dependable water in arid areas.

Public and private organizations have cooperated to construct another type of water source for wildlife in some of these water starved areas. A black asphalt or concrete apron is constructed to collect snow and rain. The moisture runs to a low point in the apron to be funnelled to an underground storage tank where evaporation is reduced. A low spot in the holding tank presents a small pond of water, about washtub sized, to thirsty wildlife. These trickle tanks (trick tanks for short) and mud tanks permit wildlife to live and prosper in areas that would otherwise be denied them.

Forest service maps, available from the district offices of the individual forests, lists most mud tanks and some trick tanks. Experienced southwestern turkey hunters know that these permanent water sources act as a magnet to fall turkeys and can keep spring turkeys clustered somewhat close. Find the water in the southwestern ponderosa pine belt and you are likely to find the turkeys.

The State of Arizona, historic Merriams range, manages its turkey flock wisely. Merriams are mostly found in the ponderosa pine belt that forests the high country. The limited habitat limits the turkeys. As is the case in many other states there are more Merriams turkey hunters than there are Merriams. Spring turkey hunting permits are allocated through a computerized lottery drawing. Permits for the fall hunt, less popular with hunters, are sold across the counter.

The hunter who hankers to take a fall Merriam's can choose from a number of turkey hunting options. The "scatter and call-back" technique used successfully in other parts of the country is seldom successful. The open terrain of much of the Merriam's range can make it difficult to creep close enough to stress the flock into a scatter. The use of turkey dogs, in almost every instance, is prohibited. A hunter who is fortunate enough to get close to a fall flock (or a spring flock for that matter) to make a scatter can call the birds back to the scatter point effectively.

Many Merriams hunters take their fall bird by ambush. The hunter finds a hide near a water source such as a stock tank or trick tank and waits for the turkeys to show. The muddy banks of the stock tanks will show if that particular tank is being used regularly by the turkeys. The kill is made with the hunters choice of legal weapons, usually a shotgun, a rifle, a bow or a muzzleloader. Fall flocks are segregated and the hunter who has picked a good spot, and has patience, can take a longbeard if that is his preference.

Ambushers who find the waterholes crowded sometimes move back into the forest to find a trail that leads from the roost or the feed grounds to the waterhole.

Hunting the feedgrounds can be a productive fall technique. Much of the Merriams range includes groves of Gambel's Oaks. Every year is not an acorn year for these oaks but when a bumper crop occurs turkeys and other wildlife such as elk, deer and black bear take advantage of the bounty. Look for characteristic turkey plowings in the leaves to find a grove that turkeys use.

Fall calling can work on Merriams, just as it does on turkeys who live in other zipcodes. The scatter/call-back technique has already been briefly alluded to. If you are fortunate and get a good scatter on a fall flock, set up at the scatter point and stay still until you hear a turkey. If the flock was a group made up of hens and the young of the year the first whistle or yelp should be heard within about one half hour. If the flock was a bachelor band of longbeards the wait may be longer, hours almost surely, and sometimes days.

The ambush can be an effective fall Merriams technique.

If the hen stays silent the assembly yelp can be effective. The series of yelps can be short or long. The author has counted a 28 yelp assembly series that took place when the flock was scattered by a hungry bobcat who had his mouth set for a taste of turkey (he ended up eating rabbit).

The kee kee whistle, the lost call of the immature turkey, can also be effective.

Some western hunters glass up feeding flocks of Merriams and stalk to rifle range.

Another fall calling technique involves locating a roost site, setting up close by before dawn, and calling in a bird after flydown. As is the case with all races of the wild turkey, gobbling is uncommon in the fall and that locator technique is not available. Although the turkeys do not often gobble in the fall they produce a lot of noisy chatter. Hens cluck back and forth as they leave the roost and as they gather on the ground. Flydown cackles are heard. Purrs are heard. Calling to a flock just after flydown can work. Merriams, in many parts of their range, roost in groves of ponderosa pine that may extend for several hundred yards. The turkeys are somewhat scattered after flydown and vocalize to get together. Listen for the sounds that the turkey makes and imitate those sounds.

The sight-em and stalk-em technique is at times a favored western technique. Hunters locate turkeys feeding in high mountain meadows, usually through binoculars, and work their way close enough to take the turkey with rifle or shotgun. That same technique is sometimes used by spring hunters as well.

Spring turkey hunting for Merriams is somewhat similar to the spring hunting of other sub-species. Hunters locate a roosting tom, if they can, then set up on that tom before daylight the next morning to call him close.

Some hunters have said that the Merriams turkey is a pushover, that the western bird is not nearly as wild and tough to call as the Eastern. Hunters who say that do so in all likelihood because it makes them feel good to think this. The "any ol sucker can kill a Merriam's but it takes a real man to tag an Eastern Syndrome." There is little doubt that individual turkeys will vary in their degree of sophistication and the degree of enthusiasm they might use to respond to the call. Being an "easy" turkey and a "tough" turkey, however, has nothing to do with the color on the tail tips. Call resistance is more likely a result of the amount of hunting pressure put on the birds. A hard hunted Merriams gets just as smart and just as call resistant as any of his Eastern cousins.

The way that a Merriams comes to a call can be influenced by the lay of the land, just as it is in other habitats. The lay of the land in Merriams range, much of the time, is chopped up canyons and semi-steep hills. A Merriams who is at Point A who hears a hunter yelp from Point B does not always walk a beeline to the call. The bird will detour around canyons and other natural obstacles to take the easiest route. The point is, do not bet all your marbles that the bird will appear from the direction of the last gobble. It is just as likely he will appear at hard right, hard left, or directly behind.

Merriam's turkeys, as a race, might be more vocal than turkeys who live in areas where the turkey population is more concentrated. Much of the Merriams habitat is marginal and turkey flocks are scattered. Bedtime gobblers sometimes holler until midnight. Daylight gobblers sometimes sound off, starting maybe a half hour before first light, until it seems they will wear out their gobble box before flydown. Some hunters allow these blabbermouth turkeys to cause them to make mistakes. Some hunters get caught up in the glory of it all, become somewhat aroused, and try to out shout the gobbler. Merriams do not always respond well to over calling. It is best to let the turkey do most of the talking with the hunter adding stingy encouragement when the tom's ardor seems to be diminishing.

A second mistake hunters sometimes make with a very vocal Merriams is to move in too close to the roost. Tom turkeys in Merriams country often roost with a grand supply of hens. Those hens, and perhaps another gobbler or two, will spread out to roost among ponderosa pine that dot a ridgeline. Trying to get too close to the loudmouth, who may be roosted in the middle or far end of the flock, can cause some of the outriders to spook. Spook one turkey in the flock and you spook them all.

Spring weather in the west can be tricky. Eastern hunters should come prepared for weather that can range from hellishly hot to damnably cold.

A number of states offer quality Merriams turkey hunting for both resident and non-resident.

Arizona, in nearly every open area, offers a quality spring Merriams hunt. The lottery allocation of permits, however, can make the hunt an iffy thing, dependent upon the whims of the computer. Hunters who apply for those areas farthest from the population centers have the best chance of being drawn. The North Kaibab National Forest is a quality hunting area and is sometimes an easy draw. So is that part of the Apache-Sitgreaves National Forest that lies along the eastern Arizona-Western New Mexico border. Across the state line, in the Gila National Forest of New Mexico, the hunting is also good, but as of this writing is not an area that requires lottery participation.

The best Merriams turkey hunting to be found in the State of New Mexico is likely the private land ranches in northern New

Mexico near the Colorado border. This high country habitat has a generous supply of water and turkey numbers are usually high. As most of the turkey hunting is on private land an access fee is charged. The access fee is usually modest if one is asking access only. If the landowner, or an outfitter, is to supply other services such as guides, food and lodging, the cost is considerably more. These are two turkey areas most years and a hunter can double his hunting pleasure at small extra cost.

The Black Hills National Forest in South Dakota (and a small part of Wyoming) offers exceptional Merriams turkey hunting. Permits are unlimited and can be bought across the counter. There is more than a million acres in the Black Hills National Forest and much of that total is turkey range. Hunters here have room to stretch out and seldom have to contend with crowds.

Many western hunters encounter primitive conditions. Larry O. Gates of Congress Arizona fills a water can from a pump on the Navajo Indian Reservation.

Hunters who decide to have a try at Black Hills turkey can extend their hunting opportunity at a small extra investment of time and funds. Wyoming, a few miles to the west, offers quality Merriams turkey hunting. So does Montana, to the west and north of the Black Hills. Some local outfitters offer package hunts that schedules a hunt in each of those three states.

An often overlooked location for quality western turkey hunts are Indian Reservations in Arizona and New Mexico.

The Hualapai (wall-ah-pie), the San Carlos Apache and the Navajo in Arizona all offer good turkey hunting opportunity. All, however, limit the number of permits and hunters are selected by a lottery drawing. Hunters who draw can count on a quality turkey hunting experience in country that is breath taking.

The Jicarilla (hick-ah-ree-ah) Apache Indian Reservation in-Northern New Mexico also offers a hunting opportunity for Merriams turkeys. Apache Indian guides are available at a moderate cost for those hunters who have a limited amount of time to devote to the hunt.

The Merriams turkey is Gould-like (or the Goulds is Merriams-like) in appearance with a lot of white on the tail tips. Both are big rangy birds that have all of the cunning needed to challenge the skill of the most experienced turkey taker. They are a worthy opponent.

Merriams hunters know that the key to finding turkey is finding water.

SELDOM SEEN TURKEYS
CHAPTER TWENTY-TWO

The Goulds sub-species of Meleagris gallopavo is the least known of the five races of that turkey. The Goulds range is almost totally confined to certain mountain ranges in Northern Mexico, although small remnant populations can be found in both Arizona and New Mexico. Meleagris gallopavo mexicana, commonly called the Goulds to honor the zoologist who described this turkey, is a mountain turkey who likely has habitat and habit similar to the traditional range of the Merriams. The tips of the tail feathers are nearly snow white, even more so than the very white of a Merriams tail tips. The white rump patch on a Goulds is not often as large as on a Merriams.

Remnant populations of the Goulds turkey remain along the United States/Mexico border in Arizona and New Mexico. (Photo Courtesy Fort Huachuca Army Base).

Hunters who have a hankering to take a Goulds must go to Mexico to do so. The small population of Goulds that are found along the United States/Mexico border in Arizona and New Mexico are carefully monitored and protected.

Hunting in Mexico requires planning, and in most instances, requires the services of a guide. A hunting trip for a Goulds turkey can be considerably simplified if the hunter depends upon the guide to supply the gun. Taking a gun in and out of Mexico requires explicit permission from Mexican officials. That small convenience, however, can be offset by the inconvenience of using a strange gun. At times, as it was when turkey calling champion Eddie Salter went to Mexico to hunt the Goulds, the gun can be very, very strange.

Eddie Salter, president of the Eddie Salter Call Company, and his right hand man Jamie Bulger flew to Chihuahua City to hunt the Goulds turkey. Because of a mixup in communication the only gun available was an antique .22 rimfire single shot rifle with a badly broken stock, somewhat repaired by wrapping the barrel to the forearm with electricians tape. Seven shells (not a lucky number as it turned out) were available. Eventually the gun problems were solved and both Eddie and Jamie were able to tag fine Goulds turkeys. Jamie's bird, with a 1 1/4" spur, earned him a place in the record book. His Goulds is listed number one for spur length.

Eddie Salter successfully hunted Goulds using a very primitive weapon.

It is better, probably, for the hunter to send his guide a letter of endorsement from a local police agency and let the guide get the necessary gun permits. The guns can be cased and checked as baggage with the airline that provides transportation. The Mexican guide makes the retrieve in Mexico.

The guide also handles licenses. Some guides offer fairly elaborate horseback hunts. One such is Enrique "Indio" Marquez of Indio Outfitters (P.O. Box 1559, Chihuahua, Chih., Mexico). Complete instructions detailing information needed for the gun permits, cost of a hunting license, how to obtain a free visa, and guide costs can be obtained by writing to Indio Outfitters at the address listed.

George Breton Maynez (Guadalupe 611 Norte, Durango, DGO-Mexico 34000) also offers guided hunts for the Goulds turkey. Those who book with George fly in to Mazatlan, then to Durango and travel to the Sierra Madre Mountains by pickup. Lance Vincent, a Florida turkey hunter who is listed in the NWTF record book as having killed the number one turkey (an Osceola), outbid the competition at the NWTF national convention in 1989 to purchase a turkey hunt for Goulds donated by George Breton Maynez and Rudolfo Gavilan. Lance did his hunting with a 70 pound draw PSE Citation, and was the first man in modern times to take a Goulds in Durango with a bow. The Goulds was a fine bird who carried a ten inch beard and ⅝" spurs. The bird is currently listed as number eight in the Goulds record book.

Here are tips that can make your hunt for a Goulds turkey more pleasant.

Guides Sam Villa and Enrique "Indio" Marquez with a pair of happy hunters, Erwin Brown of Minnesota and Ed Kohler of New York (R. to L.).

Take along a camera and plenty of film. You will be in remote country and cannot drop by the local quickstop to buy a roll of Kodachrome as needed.

Talk to your guide about your likes and dislikes in the way of food. Wilderness camps do not offer the same cuisine to be found at the Ritz, but can be surprisingly good. Even expertly prepared rib eye steak, however, can be a turnoff if you happen to be allergic to beef. Or maybe you hate broccoli (doesn't everyone?). Communication before the hunt can erase potential problems.

Talk turkey to the guide about costs, about what he is to provide and what you are to provide. Guide costs are usually negotiable. Talk to more than one to compare prices. Ask the guide to supply names and addresses of hunters who hunted with him the previous season. Contact those hunters to learn their opinion of the guide before you sign.

Inspect the material supplied by the guide to find if he is organized. The most efficient will supply information on the airlines to be used, point of departure and point of arrival, approximate cost and approximate flight time. If you notice gaps in the information supplied, correspond with the guide and ask that he send complete information.

Hunting any of the five subspecies of the North American wild turkey can be a thrill. Hunting the handsome Goulds in his home range of the Sierra Madres can be a special thrill. Done the right way, it will be a hunt that will supply memories that will last a lifetime.

Lance Vincent, who took the #1 world record turkey (an Osceola) took the #1 bow killed Goulds on a hunt guided by George Breton Maynez. (Photo from Lance Vincent files).

194

Work with a reputable outfitter. You will be hunting strange country, and unless you talk fluent Spanish, will encounter language difficulties. A guide who is familiar with the lay of the land and with local custom can be invaluable.

Talk to your doctor about that dreaded disease sometimes called The Turistas, actually a form of diarrhea caused by a breed of bug unfamiliar to the gringo digestion. You can become sick from drinking the local water or from eating certain fruits and vegetables washed in the local water. Either way, a case of the Turistas can ruin a once in a lifetime turkey hunt. It is difficult to concentrate on turkey when you are dying, or think you are. Your family physician can supply common sense advice on what not to eat or drink. He (or she) may also be able to supply medication just in case.

Gould's choose a high country habitat and a hunter who is accustomed to low country hunting might find the air a bit rarified. Goulds country, like much of the Merriams country, is a series of up and down hill climbs. Mostly up. Get in shape before the hunt. The Mexican guides will be accommodating but are not likely to carry you up and down the hills piggyback. Being in good physical shape increases your chances of tying your tag to the leg of a Goulds.

You will not be allowed to take military type guns or handguns into Mexico. Don't try to smuggle in even a small pistol "for personal protection." Mexican authorities have no sense of humor at all when it comes to handguns and autoloaders such as the AR-15, the Uzi, or even the fairly innocuous Mini- 14.

Carry a document that lists the serial number and manufacturer of each of the guns you are taking into Mexico. List the caliber or gauge and the type of action. EXAMPLE: Ithaca Model 87, 12 gauge pump action shotgun, Serial # MAG- 870025209. You will be allowed 50 rounds of ammunition per gun.

You will need six copies of a passport size photograph. Do not use an image that was taken 30 years ago when you were really good looking. A recent image, however unflattering, will be better accepted.

Arrange to carry along a certified copy of your birth certificate or a passport. If you drive into Mexico, talk to your U.S. insurance agent to learn the extent of coverage in Mexico. Even though you may have exactly the same coverage that you have in the United States, that coverage might not be the best to have in the event of an accident on the Mexican side. It may be best to arrange a short term policy with an insurance company located in Mexico. Carry your vehicle registration with you, and to be doubly safe, carry a certified copy of the title.

PRIMITIVE WEAPONS
CHAPTER TWENTY-THREE

Taking a spring or a fall turkey with a shotgun can sometimes be a chore under the best of conditions. The somewhat short range of the shotshell shooter limits shooting opportunity to about 35 yards for the 2 ¾" chambered twelve and a bit more than that for muscle guns such as the three inch twelve and the newly introduced 3 ½" twelve. Getting that close to a wary turkey, or convincing one to get that close to you, can be difficult. Even so, to a certain class of hunter, taking their tom with a shotgun is not challenging enough. Those hunters, the ones who choose to do their turkey chasing carrying a primitive weapon, compound the challenge of the spring or the fall hunt.

Early spring hunts can be timed to take advantage of bachelor band breakups, a time when gobblers are particularly desperate for female companionship. (Photo by Lovett Williams.)

The muzzle loading rifle is the least restrictive of the primitive weapons available to the turkey hunter. Antique muzzle loading rifles, and those of modern manufacture, are surprisingly accurate out to about one hundred yards. Such a weapon offers a generous increase in range over even the most modern shotgun. Most of the muzzle loading rifles offer a single shot opportunity, however, and that can force the shooter to spend that one shot wisely. Reloading

197

takes time. A measured powder charge is poured into the bore. A patched ball follows and is ramrodded home. If the rifle is a caplock a percussion cap is fitted to nipple, the hammer is cocked, and the gun is ready to fire. Elapsed time? Between 30 and sixty seconds, dependent upon the dexterity and degree of excitement.

A muzzle loader shotgun often offers two shot capability (as in the CVA Turkey Classic Double author used to take a fine Alabama Eastern) but takes about the same amount of time to recharge, in actuality, twice as much time if both barrels are reloaded.

Sure kill range is reduced. Muzzle loaders, obviously, are loaded from the muzzle. The choke that permits somewhat tight patterns is located at the muzzle. That choke, if too restrictive, can cause reloading problems. Most muzzle loader shotguns, therefore, are moderately choked. A twelve gauge gun, so choked, can deliver a killing pattern out to about 30 yards. Less is better and a lot less is a lot better.

The muzzle loader shotgun decreases range and limits shooting opportunity to one or two shots.

The bow and arrow is the most restrictive weapon available to the primitive weapon turkey hunter. Three general types of bow are currently popular. The compound bow, through a cunning cooperation of pulleys, offers much in the way of fast flat shooting.

Semi-sophisticated sight pins, coupled with practice, can cause the compound to shoot nearly as well as some rifles. There is a price to be paid for this sophistication. Compounds are a handful and can become mighty heavy if they are held at full draw for a minute or two while the shooter waits for the turkey to travel to a position that offers shot opportunity.

The longbow and the recurve, in actuality variations of the basic bow, offer lightweight but nearly none of the sophistications available with the compounds. An increasing number of "purists" are opting for either the longbow or the recurve, feeling that the taking of a turkey with either of these primitive models is a special accomplishment.

The compound bow offers excellent accuracy but can become heavy in a hurry.

The primitive limitations of all of the bows causes the taking of a spring or a fall turkey to be particularly difficult. To somewhat offset those difficulties bowhunting organizations have lobbied for and gained a special bowhunting season in many areas. The turkey bowhunt, in nearly every instance, takes place before the firearms hunt so that the archers may have the advantage of working with birds who are somewhat naive and unsophisticated. Ground or cloth blinds hide the archer from the sharp eyes of the turkey and permits him or her to draw the bow unseen. Shooting ports offer vision and shooting opportunity.

Bow hunters almost always use turkey decoys in the spring. The decoy (or decoys) can cause the bird to come close to the blind and can cause the bird to be less wary. Much of the time a passionate spring tom will strut around the decoy, presenting his fanned fanny to the archer at some point in the display. This rear view provides the archer an opportunity to aim and shoot in secrecy and offers him or her a shot at the vulnerable backbone.

Other archery sophistications are available. String trackers, a reel type device fitted to the bow and with a fine line attached to the arrow, follows the wounded turkey and aids in recovery. String silencers soften the snap of the string and sometimes make it possible to shoot repeatedly at the same gobbler. Here are tips that might make your archery hunt for turkey result in a turkey dinner.

Spring scouting is a critical element in success. If you intend to hunt from a blind (most spring archers do) it is necessary to locate an area (or areas) to construct blinds. Two turkey blinds positioned in good turkey territory is better than one. Three is better than two. Having blinds in multiple locations offers an attractive option. If the turkeys have moved out of the area where one blind is located, the hunter can move his set up to a more productive area.

Do not set the blind up on the morning you intend to hunt. It is better to construct the blind days, sometimes weeks, ahead of the hunt. This will give the turkeys time to adjust to this strange new structure. Lovesick gobblers are sometimes naive but they are seldom stupid.

Make the blind as comfortable as possible. Archers spend a long time in the blind and experienced archery hunters know that a sitting stool can be welcome furniture. A thermos of coffee can be helpful. So can a container to hold that coffee after it has been run through the system.

Using a decoy (or decoys) increases the chance of success during a spring hunt. A gobbler that comes to hen yelps expects to see a hen when he comes close. If he does not see that hen, he is not apt to hang around for long. Seeing the hen, even though it is nothing more than a spray painted piece of plastic, lets the gobbler see what he expects to see and therefore serves as a suspicion remover. The decoy gives the gobbler something to look at, something to hold his interest, while the archer prepares to do the dirty deed. Finally, the decoy has a tendency to hold the gobbler to the area of the blind long enough for the archer to take his shot, or at times, to take multiple shots.

Where you place the decoy in relation to your blind can be crucial. Veteran bow hunter Roger Raisch suggests that the decoy be placed no more than 6 yards out from the prime shooting port. Some gobblers will not come really close to the decoy. Having it close puts even that shy gobbler at risk.

Iowa archer Roger Raisch with one of the fine toms he has taken by bow. (Photo from authors files)

Schedule your hunt for the first part of the spring season, or as close to season opener as possible. Much of the time these early birds have not been educated by other hunters. Much of the time the gobblers of early spring are still in bachelor bands and are just starting to break up to mess around with the hens. There is a lot of competition between gobblers then and the archer has a good chance of calling in a desperate tom or even a gang of desperate toms. Competition has a tendency to make the tom forget that the hen is supposed to come to him.

Arrow placement must be precise if the gobbler is to be anchored. A hit anywhere along the backbone usually stops the turkey in his tracks. The backbone can be reached by a number of different routes. If the bird is facing the shooting port, head-on, aim for the place where the beard erupts from the feathers. If the bird presents a side view aim for the place where the wing butt attaches to the body. If the bird has pirouetted so that his fanned

201

tail is to the shooting port, aim for the upper center of the fan, slightly above the "pope's nose."

A fanny shot offers a good opportunity to shoot for the backbone.

A wing butt shot will sometimes anchor a gobbler.

202

Gobblers seldom drop in their tracks if the hit is less than perfect. It is not unusual for the bird to run or fly several hundred feet before he dies or brushes up. A string tracking device, mentioned earlier, provides a trail that can be followed. Make it a point to install a string tracker that has plenty of string. The Game Tracker, as an example, carries 500 yards of 22 pound line. Others may be loaded with as little as a hundred yards (or less) of line.

Two excellent books are available to help those who have a hankering to take a turkey using stick and string. Turkey Hunting Secrets (American Heritage Publishers of Iowa, 700 21st Street, West Des Moines Iowa 50265) was authored by bowhunter Roger Raisch and consists of 240 pages crammed with good advice on both archery and gun hunts. Bowhunting For Turkeys (R.D. 2, Box 2172, Bangor, PA 18013) was written by bowhunter Jack Brobst. The 131 page paperback covers many aspects on bowhunting for turkeys.

The turkey decoy lets the gobbler see what he expects to see and keeps him in the area.

TURKEYS AND CAMERAS
CHAPTER TWENTY-FOUR

The wild turkey is a grand subject for the camera. Modern color film is often challenged to accurately record all of the iridescent color shades found among the turkey's feathers. The film is challenged but almost always comes through. The image recorded on the print, or the image recorded on the transparency, is often just as handsome as the bird. That image can be retained for many years as a reinforcement for fickle memory. A photograph or a slide that is properly cared for can last several lifetimes. A photograph or a slide that is composed and exposed properly will be a valued possession for all of those lifetimes.

This pair of Rio Grande longbeards were photographed in south Texas using a 300 MM telephoto lens.

Photographing a turkey, live or dead, takes a good deal of forethought if the image is to be as good as can be. Dead turkeys are easier to compose and expose. The bird cooperates with the camera. You, as the photographer, are in total control. You can arrange pose, arrange the angle that the sun strikes the hunted and the hunter, and arrange all other aspects of the image. Even so, there are good pictures and bad pictures of the hunter and his trophy. The bad pictures, sadly, predominate.

Photographing live turkeys is immensely more difficult. The bird seldom cooperates. Turkeys are most active, almost always, during

205

that crepuscular period before the sun comes up to throw it's warming light on the subject. The click of the shutter, many times, will cause the turkey to make a desperate run for the far side of the county. As difficult as it may be, with the proper equipment, proper technique and proper dedication, nearly anyone can take decent photographs of the wild turkey. Some, perhaps more skilled or more dedicated than the others, consistently take superior photographs of the grandest game bird. The following paragraphs discuss techniques that can help. Photographing dead turkeys, being easiest, comes first.

Experienced photographers add interest by composing photos that tell a story. (Photo by Mark Kayser, South Dakota Department of Tourism).

There is a tendency for folks who are not talented photographers to view a well composed photograph and say something such as...."My, my. You must have a wonderful camera." Even though it is not meant as an insult, in actuality it is precisely that. Those critics are awarding all of the credit for photographic excellence to the instrument and none to the operator. The truth is , a person who takes the time to learn a bit about the elements that cooperate to form an excellent image can take a better than average photograph with nearly any kind of camera. That person can take an excellent photograph using any of the 35 MM cameras on the market, can take that same excellent photograph using any of the instamatics or discs, and can even do a superior job using one of the (ugh, I hate to say the word) polaroids. Here are tips that can turn your own turkey photos into an image to be displayed on the mantle rather than hid away in the darkest part of a desk drawer.

This Rio Grande turkey was called to the camera but left quickly when he couldn't find the hen.

The blame for much of the mediocre photography rests with a pair of ancient and oft repeated photo fallacies. One fallacy declares that the subject of the photograph should have the sun hitting them full in the face. The second suggests that photographs not be taken until nearly midday. Most knowledgeable photographers would just as soon take a photograph at dead midnight as they would midday. Making the subject face the sun, in most instances, produces a grimace that makes everyone look a bit like one of the California raisins with his eyes shut.

The ideal time to take photos of either dead or live turkeys is from about eight until ten in the morning and from about three to five in the evening. The sun then is low enough to fully illuminate the subject. A turkeys feathers come alive with rainbow hues. The face of the hunter, if his cap is not pulled low, is fully revealed. Even the eyes are visible. Take that same picture at noon and the angle of the sun causes the turkey feathers to go dead and causes the eyes of the hunter to disappear into the mystery of the brow shadow.

If the photograph must be taken at noon, or at any other ill advised time, compensate. Place the subject in the shade. Many modern cameras have exposure meters that automatically set shutter and aperture to match existing light. If you want to add some real snap to the photograph use a flash set to operate at about one stop above the camera lens. This will cause the subject, the proud hunter and his trophy, to stand out in stark relief. The background, being underexposed, will stay somewhat dark and inconspicuous, relinquishing all of the color and the interest to the important parts of the photo.

Photographing wild turkeys requires somewhat sophisticated equipment and a lot of pre-planning.

Get close or semi-close to the subject. Fill the viewfinder with hunter and turkey if it is a "grip and grin" sort of hero shot. Look through the viewfinder to search out any distractions such as empty beer cans (even full ones), once used pampers, or any other woods trash. Sit the happy hunter next to something scenic. Perhaps a weathered wood stump. Perhaps a blooming dogwood. Use your eyes and your imagination to discover the best possible setting.

Spend an equal amount of thought on the pose. Do not allow the hunter (either yourself or a companion) to stand slack-jawed with a Jack Nickolson sneer and a half smoked Pall Mall hanging obscenely from one side of the mouth, perhaps holding the magnificent wild turkey by the neck as if he was choking a chicken. Such a pose shows little respect for the turkey and none for the hunter.

It is better to sit the hunter in front of a non-intrusive background, place the turkey in front of him with wings spread and tail fanned. Allow the bird, even dead, to retain dignity. And have the hunter smile. This should be a happy moment and the camera should reflect that happiness. Too many times the hunter faces the camera with a scowl that seems to say "I've finally killed this sucker and now I'm gonna go out and get me another'n".

A number of poses look well on film. Shoulder the bird to simulate the pack out, carrying the turkey by the feet. Place the turkey on a log or a stump with wings spread and tail fanned and position yourself (happily) alongside.

In every instance take the time to wipe away any blood that may have soiled the turkey head. Slightly moistened toilet tissue works well.

Turkey hunters who hope to capture a wild live turkey on film need a bit more specialized equipment. A 35 MM camera SLR (single lens reflex) is nearly mandatory. Select one that permits the lens to be changed as conditions warrant.

The cost of such cameras can vary as options vary. Nearly all of the major camera manufacturers offer SLR's that are nearly totally automatic. Pressing a button causes the lens to automatically focus on the subject. Pressing that button a bit more causes the camera to automatically set shutter speed and aperture and to activate the shutter. Buy the best camera you can afford. Prorate the cost over a lifetime of use and even the best is a bargain.

A telephoto lens will be needed. A 70-210 MM zoom might suffice. Lenses with more magnification, either a 300MM, a 400 MM or even a 500 MM might be better. The more powerful lenses usually do not deliver sharp images if they are hand held and a tripod may be necessary.

Some hunting lodges maintain no-hunt sanctuaries for the benefit of photographers (Photo taken on the Kennedy Ranch in south Texas).

Seek out a place where turkeys congregate in a sanctuary situation if possible. Many landowners encourage the visit of wild turkey flocks by bribing them with corn and other edibles. Inquire around to find such a place and ask permission to visit. Parks and refuges are other options. Even though these somewhat docile birds are totally wild, habituation has caused them to tolerate a reasonably close approach.

Plan the photography outings to take advantage of the most propitious shooting times, early morning and late afternoon. Position the camera at a low angle, a turkey eye view as it were, to make the bird look as grand as he is and to catch the full benefit of the play of light upon the feathers.

The choice of film is a personal matter. Kodak's TRi-X (ASA 400) is a good choice in the black and whites. Kodak's Kodachrome 25 and 64 are the standard by which other slide films are measured. Kodak's Ektar and Kodacolor each deliver excellent color prints.

If you are unable to locate a sanctuary to do the turkey filming, the task of wild turkey photography is made considerably more difficult but it can be done. Find a secluded area that shows evidence of turkey activity and select a site that offers the vision and light needed for photography. Construct a ground blind or purchase one of the factory mades. Use corn or other grain to convince the birds to come to that site on a somewhat regular schedule. Check with the game managers in your state to learn of regulations that may apply to such baiting. Give the turkeys several days, maybe weeks, to become accustomed to the blind before you move in. Experienced photographers place the bottom of a soft drink bottle into the shooting port so that the turkeys will not be alarmed when the glassy eye of the telephoto lens peers out to record their movements.

Do not do your baiting and photography in areas you plan to hunt. It is considered tacky (and illegal) to bait the turkeys to the camera and then move in on opening day to turn hostile. Do not permit your brother-in-law to do so either. Such unsportsmanlike behavior can cause the local game protector to take an intense interest in your activities from that point until the day you die.

Bait or a decoy can cause spring gobblers to hang around the area. (Photo by Mark Kayser, South Dakota Department of Tourism).

Some hunting lodges reserve sanctuaries for the benefit of the wildlife photographer. Modest fees are usually the rule as this type of customer is non-consumptive. They remove nothing from the land. Many times such photo-only areas are baited and blinds are provided.

Examine the classified advertisements in magazines like The Turkey Hunter, Turkey Call, Outdoor Photographer (Box 57213, Boulder, CO 80322-7213), and even more generalized outdoor publications to discover sources.

The photographing of the wild turkey, it should be noted, is almost always a difficult endeavor requiring specialized equipment and dedication. Do not expect to grab your Instamatic on a Sunday afternoon to head to the woods for a satisfying session of wildlife photography.

Some photographers attempt to make turkey photography less difficult by aiming their cameras at one of the local fifty pound butterballs. Those photographs are easy to obtain. If you want a great picture of a tame turkey, go to it. You will have a tough time, however, convincing knowledgeable turkey takers that the bird is anything more than a barnyard fowl who has had every ounce of wildness bred from his genes.

Taking great photos of dead turkeys requires a bit of forethought but can be simply done using very basic equipment. Taking great photographs of live one hundred percent gold plated wild turkeys is more difficult and requires specialized equipment and dedication. In either instance, however, the product produced is ample reward.

Using a fill-in flash, even during daylight, can add snap to photos like this one of Wisconsin turkey hunter Pat Akey, advertising manager for Turkey Hunter Magazine.

FIELD CARE
CHAPTER TWENTY-FIVE

Prehunt scouting, skillful calling and luck can cause a trophy tom to come to the setup. The most exciting part of the hunt is seconds away. The turkey displays twenty five yards out and pirouettes, turning so that his fanned tail hides his patriotic head. You take this opportunity to raise the shotgun to the shoulder and place the barrel bead about where you think the head should be. You wait, tense with excitement, until the strutter turns to face the gun. A sharp putt with the double reeded diaphragm causes the tom to raise his head high, looking for danger. The barrel bead drops halfway between the root of the paint brush beard and the top of the head and you stroke the trigger. In a heartbeat the tom is on the ground. You quickly chamber a fresh round, put the gun on safe, and hurry to the tom. Your hunt has ended.

Calling a strutter close for a sure shot ends one part of the turkey hunt but is the start of a second part.

Every statement in the preceding paragraph excepting the last sentence could be true. Each year thousands of spring hunters play out a scenario that approximates the circumstances described. The last sentence, however, is seldom true. The opera ain't over until the fat lady sings and the hunt is not over at the sound of the shot. One part of the hunt remains. That twenty pounds of meat, bone, guts and feathers must be turned into something that is edible, mountable or both. Here are some of the steps taken by experienced hunters after the adrenalin ebbs and the echoes of the shot have ended.

It is important to immediately chamber a live round if your turkey getter is not an auto loader. A turkey that goes down hard at the shot is not always one hundred percent dead, or as some southerners put it, graveyard dead. Some turkeys have been know to enjoy a miraculous recovery. Having a fresh round in the chamber can be good insurance.

It is tempting to run as hard as you can to the turkey for a laying on of the hands (actually the feet). Make your gun safe before starting the trip. Even then, do not run to the carcass as if a hungry grizzly was hot on your heels. Proceed at a brisk and safe walk, carrying your gun at the ready as you make the approach.

Take a moment to admire and photograph the turkey before thinking seriously about field care.

When you are certain that the turkey has breathed his last take a moment to admire your trophy. Then immediately tie on your tag to make the kill legal. If you don't do it now it will be easy to forget later. Use your camera to record the moment for memory. Lay aside your gun, your camera and your calls and get started on the job of preparing the turkey for the trip to the taxidermist or the trip to the kitchen.

If the turkey is to be mounted, and if the day is cool, if the taxidermist is a short drive distant, you may need do nothing to the turkey before transport. Refer to the suggestions contained in the chapter on turkey taxidermy to discover options.

If the turkey is to be an eating turkey, as most are, the hunter is faced with a number of choices. He or she can transport the bird as is if the journey is to be short. The job of field dressing the fowl, then skinning or plucking as individual preference suggests, is easiest done if cold or hot water is available.

If the drive home will take time, or if the weather is warm, take the time needed to remove the intestines and other organs from the body cavity. Turkey are like quail in at least one respect. It is difficult to understand how something that tastes so good can smell so bad. Leaving the fecal matter within the intestines inside the warm body cavity can cause a smell that will call buzzards and blow flies from an amazing distance.

Slice through the muscle of the gizzard to remove the inner pouch and contents.

To draw the bird use the point of the knife to make a slit that extends from the rim of the vent to the point of the breast. Reach in to grasp the intestines and pull them out. If you possess what is sometimes called a nervous stomach, and if the thought of placing a strangle hold on that mass of slimy guts causes you to seriously consider tossing your waffles, you might wish to carry a set or two of vinyl gloves in your pack. These can be found at many pharmacies and are available in a variety of sizes. Ask for Single Use Vinyl Examination Gloves.

One intestine, the anal gut, will remain attached to the vent. Use the knife to cut the rim of the vent away from the body and discard it with the gut. Reach farther up into the body cavity and grasp the heart, the gizzard and the liver if they did not come out with the first hand full. Place these organs into a ziplock bag carried for that purpose. Each of these organs can be a tasty treat when properly prepared.

Both the heart and the gizzard need a bit of help before they are ready to be placed in the pot. Cut the heart open to expose the chambers and wash out the residual blood. Hold the gizzard so that one edge is available to the knife and slice through the muscle just far enough to expose the distinctive grey membrane that protects the gizzard stones and food. Peel the red muscle away from the grey sack. After washing the gizzard will be ready for the pot.

Washing out the body cavity cleans the turkey and hastens cooling.

Use your fingers to feel up to the very end of the body cavity to discover the lungs and pull them loose from the wall of the cavity. Go to the "V" of the breast to discover the crop and it's contents. Make a slit in the skin and remove this food storage pouch.

If water is available use it to flush out the body cavity to clean and cool it. If snow is available, stuff a Ziplock bag with the snow and place the bagged snow up into the body cavity to hasten cooling.

There are two ways to prepare a turkey for the cooker. One is by skinning and the second is by plucking. Skinners do so because it is a fast and easy way to disrobe a turkey. If you consider yourself to be a skinner, you may wish to complete that job before leaving the woods. The breast and the legs are the main edibles on a wild turkey and they take up minimal space in the ice chest. Some hunters, particularly those who intend to be in camp for a day or two before returning home, bone out each side of the breast to hasten cooling and further conserve ice chest space.

To skin the turkey tie one or both feet to a limb and use your fingers to tear the feathered skin away from the flesh. The cut made to access the entrails is a good place to start. Use a trash bag carried for that purpose to hold unwanted parts. This serves a pair of purposes. It keeps the woods somewhat clean and it provides a handy container for parts that you may wish to salvage. Parts like the tail fan, the wings, the lower legs and the beard. Even the turkey feathers can be utilized if you happen to be a fisher who ties flies, or if you have such a person among your circle of friends.

The turkey skin is tender when the bird is freshly dead and the skin will come away in large tears. When the skin and the feathers have been removed (don't worry at this point if a few feathers cling to the flesh) use the knife to cut the breast away from the back. Cut off the wings at the joint and cut off the legs (check local regulations before removing the tagged leg. You may be required to leave this on the turkey until you reach home. Some regulations may also require the beard to stay on the carcass of a spring turkey until transport is complete).

Many turkey hunters save the spurs, the beard and the tail of the turkeys they take. The spurs can be removed by using a hack saw to cut through the leg bone a half inch or so on each side of the spur. Remove the beard by cutting a silver dollar sized patch of skin and feathers away with it. Remove the tail by cutting through the bottom of the button (sometimes called the "Pope's Nose"). Many hunters like to leave a flap of back skin attached.

When the breast and the legs have been removed from the rest of the turkey, if water is available, wash away the feathers that have stuck to the flesh and refrigerate for the trip home.

217

If regulations permit remove the beard by cutting away a silver dollar size patch of skin & feathers.

If you decide to be a plucker you may be able to dry pluck the bird at the kill site. Dry plucking can be a chore. Hang the bird by the head at a comfortable working height. Pull the feathers away from the body in the direction they grow. Put another way, if the turkey is hanging by his feet, pull up on the feathers. Pulling down will almost surely tear the skin. Do not become overly ambitious and attempt to tear too big a bunch of feathers at one grab. The plucking job can turn into a skinning job quickly.

Continue to pluck until the turkey has been defeathered. Cut off the wings and the head. Make the vent slit and remove the entrails and organs. Make another slit to remove the crop and pull away the crop and it's contents. You will notice a foul looking deposit of fat within the "V" of the breast. This is called the sponge and is an accumulation of fat that sustains the gobbler through the rigors of the breeding season. Many turkey hunters leave this fatty deposit on the bird as they feel that the sponge delivers a tasty basting to the turkey as it cooks.

Wet plucking is much easier and faster than the dry method but can seldom be done in the field. Transport the bird home ungutted if the trip is short. Otherwise remove the entrails and organs and fill the body cavity with ice or snow if it is available. Lay the bird in the coolest part of the vehicle (this is not the fender) and drive directly home. Resist the temptation to haul the carcass on a tour of several counties to display the trophy to relatives, friends and schoolmates you have not seen for twenty years.

A pair of experts can wet pluck a turkey in a matter of minutes. On a recent Alabama hunt with Eddie Salter and CVA President Bob Hickey the author was privileged to watch two such experts,

Willie Clyde and Miss Sadie Marshall, cooperate to pluck a wild turkey gobbler. It took them six minutes. Here is the way they went about it.

Willie Clyde and Miss Sadie Marshall of Andalusia, Alabama with the six minute turkey.

Miss Sadie heated enough boiling water to cover the turkey in a medium wash tub. If this is not possible heat enough water to wet half the turkey at a time. Add a couple of tablespoons of liquid detergent to the water. Turkey feathers are coated with a natural oil, soaping permits the feathers and the skin that holds them to be scalded.

Hold one end of the turkey by the feet and the opposite end by the head. Immerse the bird in the hot water and leave it there for a half a minute or so. If there is only enough water to scald half the turkey, rotate the bird so that the entire carcass is scalded.

Remove the turkey from the water and use gloved hands (that sucker is hot) to pull out the feathers by the handful. As with dry plucking, pull with the grain of the feathers to avoid tearing.

Finish off in the way described for dry plucking. Take the plucked bird to the sink (or the hose) and rinse away all traces of the soapy water.

Wild turkeys are good eating and they are good for you, having much less fat and nasty old cholesterol than domestic strains. Handled right, skinned or plucked, the bird will provide a meal that will tempt the most jaded appetite.

TURKEY TAXIDERMY
CHAPTER TWENTY-SIX

Bob Peers of Phoenix Arizona is one taxidermist who does his turkey the old fashioned way. He takes his time at every step, doing all he can to correct the damage sometimes done by careless handling in the field. There are times, Bob admits, when mounting strutters and flyers is a tough way to make a living. His job, he claims, would be a lot easier if hunters took the time to handle the bird correctly in the field. Bob and Pat Peers are the husband and wife owners of Quail Run Taxidermy.

Hunters who develop a hankering to have a turkey mounted, Bob believes, would be well advised to take that turkey during the spring season. Many fall turkeys have pin feathers that need time to grow. By spring, the bird has weathered a tough or semi- tough winter. Every feather has had ample time to mature. Mounts of spring toms will look bigger and will be more full bodied.

Many taxidermists offer a touch up service at a moderate cost.

The hunter's choice of a turkey taker can make the difference between a majestic mount and one that is about half that. Once or twice each season a hunter packs in a carcass that has been cannoned. Shot with the trusty thirty thirty. Shot with an ought six. Shot with a seven mag. Shot with a rifle that is bored to deliver one shot kills on Kodiaks or moose. As tactfully as he can, trying not to hurt their feelings, Bob explains there is not enough turkey left to mount. Maybe a beard plaque? Maybe a fan board? Next year, he suggests mildly, leave the centerfire in the gun safe and take the turkey with a smoothbore. Load that puppy with bird shot, sixes or seven and a halfs, and aim for the head or the neck.

When a turkey hits the deck, most hunters know they must get on him in a hurry to prevent a miraculous recovery. A flopping turkey is a turkey with some life left. A turkey with the least iota of life just might enjoy a fast run for the county line, taking the hunters turkey dinner along for the ride.

Hunters who hope to have the bird mounted have a second reason for getting on the turkey in a hurry. The flopping dislodges more than a few feathers and every loss can leave a gap in the turkey overcoat. Get on the bird fast, Bob advises, and as well as you can, avoiding spurs and claws, hold the bird immobile until the last bit of life leaves. When the bird is 100% dead pick up any dropped feathers and bag them for the trip to the taxidermist. A skilled taxidermist can use those sheds to fill the gaps.

When that job is done use small plugs of paper toweling or toilet tissue to plug the natural and unnatural holes in the carcass. Blood can seep from the wounds. Blood and body fluids can creep from the body cavities. Both will soil and sometimes stain the feathers of an otherwise perfect mount.

The time to contact a taxidermist is as far before the hunt as possible. Some taxidermists may not do turkeys. Others may have contracted for all of the turkey they can fit into their schedule. Some might charge more than you can afford to pay. Hunting down a taxidermist and working out all of those details while carrying a hot turkey in your hands can be a bummer. Find your taxidermist during the calm before the hunt. Work out price and the kind of mount desired.

If you happen to hunt close to the town where the taxidermist has his shop, and if the weather is cold, you may not need to remove the intestines before you transport. If you feel that you should, or if the transport will take some time, slip the point of your knife blade into the vent and make about a four inch cut toward the point of the breastbone. Slip your hand into the body cavity to grasp and draw out the intestines and the organs. Use more toweling to plug the body cavity and gently remove any blood or fluids that may have soiled the feathers.

Cold weather transportation can be simple. You may need only put the carcass into a large plastic bag to keep off dust. If you must travel a great distance, or if the weather is warm, it is a good policy to ice the carcass before transport. Place the bird into a clean 30 gallon trash bag, tie the top shut, and place the bird gently on a layer of ice. Take care that the feathers are not wetted as the ice melts.

Cooling can be hastened by placing a zip lock bag filled with ice into the body cavity.

If it is not possible to take the bird directly to the taxidermist because of the distance involved or because of the day of the week, take the bird to your home and place the bagged bird into a large chest type food freezer if one is available. Once frozen the bird will keep for many months without noticeable deterioration.

Most hunters have an interest in the work and material that can turn a turkey into a mount. Although all taxidermists have their own semi-secret tricks of the trade, most follow a more or less standard procedure.

The bird is skinned by extending the vent slit almost to the top of the breast bone. The hide is gently pulled from the body and generous amounts of preservative, maybe borax, is added to the flesh side of the skin as it is removed. The borax soaks up body fluids that might otherwise soil the feathers.

What of the meat? The job of the taxidermists is made less difficult if you agree to eat the meat of a butterball for your Thanksgiving dinner. For those who insist on eating their turkey and having it too, cornmeal or cornstarch can be substituted for the borax. Either of those substitutes do nearly as well as the borax as a dryer. There is one small problem. Bugs that love turkey hides but hate borax also love cornmeal and cornstarch. Without the bugproofing borax, the mount may end up making a meal for a horde of hungry dermestid beetles.

The feet come off with the hide. There is little there to taint so they are left essentially as is. The folds of skin around the head are split and cured. The skull is cleaned and laid aside for later use. Bird mounts and a very few animals, are mounted using the natural skull. Others are mounted using a plastic skull replica.

Taxidermists now have a number of options when it comes time to mount a turkey's head. Skinning out the head and then refitting skin to the skull, the technique Bob uses, is one way. Another way involves the use of a plastic replica of the head as a substitute. Each replica is individually painted by the taxidermist.

Freeze drying the unskinned head is another option. Freeze dried heads, much of the time, look more natural than either of the techniques described. The bad news? The freeze drying technique is the most expensive.

After skinning, the turkey hide is re-boraxed for extra protection and a body form is made from paper maiche or shredded wood.

The skin is fitted around the form and sewed shut with black thread. Wire supports are added to the wings for flying mounts. Feathers, feet and wattle are given a final touch-up and the mount is finished.

The head is the most difficult part of the turkey mount. Ask to see examples of the taxidermist's work.

The finished mount is nothing more than the turkey hide, body stuffing, and a bit of borax. Peers has a hard time, on occasion, convincing a hunter's wife that there isn't still a turkey in there somewhere.

Proper care of the mount in the home can add years to the "life" of the mounted bird. Sunlight can cause the feathers to fade. Dust and grease contamination are common. Bugs are bad. Watch for the "rice crispy like" shell of the common carpet beetle. Those little boogers like turkey hide about as well as they do carpet. Maybe better.

When you find carpet beetle evidence you can bet your last load of birdshot the critter is hot on the heels of your turkey. Put the bird and a pest strip into a large trash bag, tie shut the top, and let the two coexist for a couple of weeks.

Other dangers? Would you believe household pets? Bob spent a good deal of his time one spring making a double strut mount of a pair of handsome gobblers. He apparently did too good a job. A few months after delivery a sad faced man came to the shop carrying the big pieces of the grand double strutter. For weeks, he sobbed, Tabby had been intently watching the turkeys. Tabby would arch his back and growl to show his hostility each time he passed by the unconcerned gobblers. One evening, as cat and master sat reading the paper (not Tabby...cats can't read) the feline made a giant leap to land on the back of the easy chair, bounced to the mantle, and groaning horribly began a slashing attack on the unsuspecting gobblers.

A strutting mount can be spectacular but is often the most expensive option.

Tabby and the turkeys fell to the floor in a flurry of fur and feathers. The bottom line? It cost the hunter a hundred and a half to restore some dignity to the mount.

The hunter paid glumly and headed for the door carrying the restored mount. He paused, Columbo-like, to throw back a last comment. "Say Bob", he asked conversationally, "do you do cats?"

Dogs can be nearly as hard on mounts as cats. Maybe more so. Bob still chuckles when he recalls the wife who contracted to have her husband's turkey mounted as a Christmas present. She placed the strutting bird under the tree on Christmas Eve and turned in, confident that her hubby was in for the surprise of his life. He got it. So did she. They awoke the next morning to find turkey feathers, borax and excelsior scattered from wall to wall. The family cocker lay in the middle of the mess, looking tired but happy.

The beard taken from a turkey gobbler can be a pleasant reminder of the hunt. Use a knife to cut up from the underside of the beard, skinning out a dollar bill sized (or a twenty dollar bill sized if you are really flush) patch of skin with feathers and beard attached. Carefully scrape off excess fat and rub on preservative. Tack the feathers and beard to a board for drying.

Many hunters also remove the spurs from their trophy. Gobblers begin to grow "button" spurs during the first year of growth and the spurs continue to grow throughout the turkey's life. Spurs longer than one inch are considered to be from a trophy turkey. The spur is actually a horny growth (similar to the human fingernail) that is supported by a core of bone. Although spurs can vary, most are black. A few gobblers (very few) have multiple spurs.

To remove the spur use a hacksaw to cut through the leg bone about a quarter of an inch above and below the spur. Use your knife to cut the scaly skin away from the legbone. Scrape away flesh and tendons. Use a nail to punch out the bone marrow. Let the bone and spur dry and use sandpaper or steel wool to remove all traces of flesh or gristle. Paint the bone with a clear varnish of glossy white paint if desired. A number of spurs can be strung on a leather throng to make an attractive necklace, often with a turkey beard as the center decoration.

A hunter who is considering having a turkey mounted should stop to consider that few taxidermists have the skill needed to deliver a life like mount of a turkey gobbler. It is good practice to ask to see examples of the turkey taxidermists work before handing over the turkey. Ask also for names and numbers of previous customers. Call them to verify satisfaction.

A visit to taxidermy competitions like the one held annually by the NWTF can provide insight into taxidermy excellence. (Ocellated turkey shown).

If the budget allows, attend one of the National Wild Turkey Federation conventions. A taxidermy contest is usually a part of the program. Look over the entries and make a note of those that do an impressive job.

Turkey taxidermy can be expensive. A poorly 17 executed mount can be the most expensive because money has been wasted on an inferior product. The cost, the way Bob Peers sees it, is little enough to pay to preserve the memory of an exciting hunt. Maybe the motto printed over his shop door says it best. "The quality is remembered long after the price is forgotten."

Another hunter kept his tom on a lamp table, close at hand so that he could stroke it as the urge developed. He returned from an afternoon of quail hunting one afternoon trailed by his faithful German Short Haired Pointer. The GSP saw the bird & locked into a classic three legged point that was aimed straight at the regal turkey. Seconds later he charged and retrieved, laying the bird proudly at his master's feet.

The best bet for display, Bob thinks, is to put the critter under glass. If that is not possible, regular attention with a feather duster will move the surface dust around a bit. You may wish to put the vacuum on blow to use that gentle flow of air to remove more dust. When the mount begins to look ratty, really dirty, make a return trip to the taxidermist. He can restore the bird to original beauty for a modest charge.

Most taxidermy studios offer a variety of mount options. The strutter is popular. The price will vary as the zip code of the taxidermist changes. A flying or standing mount is less costly. Other options are even less expensive. Hunters who have spent a wad on the hunt and who consequently have a cold wind blowing through their bank account might opt for an inexpensive beard mount or for a plaque that holds the fanned tail, the head and the beard.

A few minutes of work permits the hunter to turn the tail of his turkey into a handsome wall decoration.

Even the most hard core turkey addict does not have every turkey tagged mounted. At least most don't. Nearly all, however, keep some part of the trophy as a remembrance of the hunt. The fanned tail feathers can be easily prepared and preserved. Some hunters leave a part of the feathered back skin attached. Here is how it is done.

Use a sharp knife to cut the underside of the "pope's nose" (actually an oily organ that provides waterproofing for the feathers) away from the body. Cut a four or five inch long strip of back skin (with feathers attached) if you wish to do so. Work from the underside of the "pope's nose" and scrape away as much of the fatty tissue as possible. Rub a preservative such as borax onto the remaining skin. Tack the fanned tail to a board or to a wall and allow it to dry.

Some companies (San Angelo Manufacturing, 909 West 14th Street, San Angelo TX 76903 is one) make and market a tail mounting plaque that has room for the beard.

One or both of the turkey wings can be preserved in about the same way. Make a slit in the skin on the side that will be against the wall and remove as much meat as possible. Rub in preservative. Use a hypodermic needle (available at pharmacies) to inject a liquid preservative into the joints. Tack the spread wing onto wood or a wall to dry.

Companies like San Angelo offer plaque kits that hold both tail fans and beards.

TURKEY ON THE TABLE
CHAPTER TWENTY-SEVEN

Every turkey hunter, nearly, is sincere about the hunt for the biggest bird that flies. Some, (maybe even most) are fanatical. They will leave a warm bed, leave a warm wife, well before first light to make the long and lonely drive to the ridge. Most do not complain about wet bottoms, mosquitos, chiggers, ticks and others of the same persuasion. When the tom is tagged, however, when he has been brought home for all of his neighbors (some living as far away as Chicago) to admire, most lose interest in the process that turns the tom from a mess of feathers, muscle & meat into something good to eat. The turkey hunters' wives, bless 'em every one, take over to turn that turkey into something that is worth sinking a tooth into.

Talented turkey cooks like Cindy Peterson of Flagstaff Arizona can turn a trophy into a dish that tickles the taste buds.

Every cook who works with wild turkey meat has her (or his) own favorite way of frying, baking, basting, grilling or jerking the wild turkey. The paragraphs that follow list the favorite recipe of some high profile turkey hunters followed by a few of the authors own favorites.

J.C. Brown sure qualifies as a dedicated turkey hunter. This Mississippi hunter has worked as a right hand man to Allen Jenkins, head man at the M.L. Lynch Company, the folks that make those great box calls. J.C.'s wife Dorcas gets to do so much wild game cooking she has written a book on the subject. Camouflage Cuisine is a hundred page paperback crammed with taste tempting recipes (Camouflage Cuisine, P.O. Box 1297, Woodville MS 39669). Here is Dorcas' favorite way to cook turkey breast:

TURKEY BREAST IN MUSHROOM SAUCE

Bone out the breast of a wild turkey and salt & pepper to taste and place the breast in a shallow baking dish. Stir together 1 can of cream of mushroom soup, 1 tablespoon dried parsley, 2 tablespoons of dried beef slices (chopped), 1 teaspoon thyme and one small bunch of chopped green onions. Bake 1 hour in 350 degree oven.

Dorcas Brown, shown here with husband J.C., is such a good wild game cook she has written a book on the subject.

ROAST WILD TURKEY

Pluck the turkey, remove the entrails and wash clean. Stuff with ½ stick of butter (or margarine) 2 medium skinned onions, and 2 medium peeled apples. Close the opening. Salt & pepper the bird and lay on 4 strips of bacon. Place 1 teaspoon of flour and spices of choice into cooking bag and insert turkey. Shake to coat with the flour & close the bag. Roast breast down at 325-350 for 15-25 minutes a pound. Turn turkey breast up for last 30 minutes of cooking.

MONSTROUSLY GOOD FRIED TURKEY

Sprinkle 15-20 pound turkey with salt, black pepper and red pepper, inside and out. Place in heavy duty foil in a deep pan. Pour on a dressing made of 3 tablespoons or more of hot pepper sauce, 1-16  ounce bottle of Italian dressing and 5 tablespoons of Worcestershire sauce (for a variation, sauce may be injected into the turkey). Close the foil around the turkey and refrigerate for several hours. Remove from the 'frige 30 minutes before cooking. Cook, using an outdoor burner heating a large pot with a basket. The grease or oil (about 5 gallons needed) should be very hot. Place turkey in the basket and lower it into the hot oil. Cook 3 minute per pound turning carefully several times during cooking. The turkey should be crisp on the outside and juicy on the inside. Serve with potatoes prepared as follows: Wash and quarter 20 pounds of potatoes and marinate in the turkey sauce, stirring to coat evenly. When the turkey has been removed from the cooking basket put potatoes in and cook until done, testing with fork after potatoes are lightly browned. Remove and serve.

Geri Jenkins fries her turkeys whole to produce a monstrously good meal.

Geri Jenkins is another lady who has ties to the M.L. Lynch Company. As the wife of Allen Jenkins, Geri works very hard helping Allen run the company. She also gets a lot of practice cooking wild turkeys and works just as hard at that. Geri and Allen like their turkey fried, but prefer it fried in one grand lump. Here is the way Geri Jenkins fries her turkeys:

TURKEY JERKY

Cut skinned and boned turkey breast into ⅛" strips. Cut with the grain. Make a seasoning of 1 tablespoon garlic salt, 1 tablespoon black pepper, ¼ teaspoon of cayenne pepper and 1 teaspoon of salt. Sprinkle the seasoning on the turkey strips and place in glass dish and refrigerate overnight. Place strips across oven rack leaving oven door slightly open to release moisture. Bake at low heat (125 degrees) for 4 hours or until meat is thoroughly dried. Take along on your next turkey scout or turkey hunt as trail food.

Shirley Grenoble tags her turkey, cooks it, and then writes up the hunt to sell to a national magazine.

SMOKIN' HOT SMOKED TURKEY

Place the cleaned turkey in a deep roasting pan and check to be sure the hood of your barbecue pit will close over it. Fill the cavity of the turkey with ½" of dry white wine. When charcoal has burned down add chips of hickory wood. Combine 1 pound butter or margarine, 1 cup lemon juice, 1 cup Worcestershire sauce, 1 tablespoon soy sauce, 1 tablespoon of salt and ⅛ teaspoon of Tabasco sauce. Bring to a slow boil and add 1 cup of dry sherry. Cook turkey 4-6 hours basting frequently with the sauce.

Shirley Grenoble of Altoona, Pennsylvania, is a turkey hunter as well as a turkey cook. Many turkey hunters know her best through the job she held as a national director for the National Wild Turkey Federation. Shirley is also an outdoor writer who has been published many times in *The Turkey Hunter,* as well as other nationally distributed outdoor magazines. Shirley likes to smoke her turkey. Here is the way she goes about it.

BUTSKI FRIED TURKEY BREAST

Remove the turkey breast from the bone and slice cross-grain. Dip each piece into a mixture made of 1 cup buttermilk and 1 egg. Season with salt and pepper (to taste) and coat each piece with flour. Deep fry in hot oil until browned.

Phyllis Loadholtz has been a turkey hunter's wife for many years. Her husband Doyle has been honored for his hard work with the National Wild Turkey Federation. Doyle and Phyllis hang out in Lake City, Florida. Doyle has hunted the wild turkey in many states. Doyle and Phyllis like their turkey breast fried also. Here is one way Phyllis keeps Doyle from turning too skinny.

Halina Butski is another turkey hunter wife who gets lots of practice cooking wild turkeys. Halina's husband Paul consistently wins in turkey calling contests (he has won the world championship) and is a hard hunter. Halina and Paul prefer their turkey fried.

Tom Yacovella is a turkey hunter and an artist who lives in New York State. Here is Joanne Yacovella's recipe for turning turkey breast into a delicious meal.

BAKED TURKEY STRIPS
Cut breast meat of the wild turkey into strips. Brush strips with olive oil and broil for 3-5 minutes. Preheat oven to 300 degrees. Line pan with strips of meat and sprinkle with two packages of dry onion soup mix. Add one cup water and two cups wine or beer. Cover with aluminum foil and bake for 2 ½ hours. Serve over noodles or rice.

Being able to have your fun and eat it too is one of the great advantages found in being a turkey hunter. Here are other recipes that could cause your salivary glands to work overtime.

Joanne Yacovella likes her turkey in strips.

FRIED TURKEY FILETS

Partially freeze the turkey breast to make it easy to slice and cut it into ½" thick slices (cross grain). Salt and pepper the slices and layer them in a pan. Let them set for a few minutes and then flour each piece. Fry in hot oil or grease until just brown. Do not overcook as the secret to tenderness is fast cooking.

Tom Yacovella is a turkey hunter and an artist who lives in New York State. Here is Joanne Yacovella's recipe for turning turkey breast into a delicious meal.

WILD TURKEY & WILD RICE

Cut one side of boned turkey breast into serving-sized pieces. Mix together ½ cup white rice, ½ cup wild rice, 1 can cream of mushroom soup, 1 can cream of chicken soup and 1 cup water. Add rice and pour into 9"x13" aluminum cake pan. Lay turkey pieces on top. Cover with aluminum foil and bake for 4 hours at 275 degrees. Remove foil for last 15 minutes to brown.

FRIED TURKEY BREAST

Bone each side of the breast from a wild turkey. Cut away the skin. Slice the breast filets cross-grain into steaks about ½" thick. Marinate overnight in a marinade made of 1 can evaporated milk, 2-3 cloves of crushed garlic, season salt & pepper to taste.

When ready to cook remove steaks from marinate and roll in flour. Fry in hot cooking oil about three minutes to a side.

TURKEY OLE'

Boil ½ a turkey boned turkey breast (1 side) with one cup chopped green onions, 1 cup chopped celery and salt to taste for 30 minutes. Cool and cut meat into bite size chunks. Combine one 4-ounce can Ortega chopped chiles, 2 cans cream of mushroom soup, ½ cup milk, ½ cup sour cream, ½ cup chopped onion and one cup grated monterey jack cheese (or your choice). Combine with one dozen broken tortillas. Bake 20 minutes at 350. Add a cup of grated cheese to the top and sprinkle with a half cup of chopped green onions. Return to oven until cheese melts, about 10 minutes.

CHILI GREEN

Cut left over roast turkey breast into bite size chunks. Mix 1 chopped onion (medium), 1 clove chopped or crushed garlic, 1 cup canned tomatoes and 1 can Ortega chiles. Add salt, pepper & oregano to taste. Heat in a skillet until hot. Add meat and enough hot water to cover. Simmer for 30 minutes. Sprinkle in flour to thicken. Roll in flour tortillas to serve. Or if preferred, brown the tortilla rolled mixture in hot oil to turn to chimichangas.

WET & WILD JERKY

Skin & bone wild turkey breast. Cut with the grain into ¼" strips. Make marinate of 1 tsp liquid smoke, ⅓ tsp garlic powder, 1 tsp onion powder, ¼ cup soy sauce, ¼ cup Worcestershire sauce, ½ tsp black pepper and 1 tsp Mono Sodium Glutamate. Marinate meat for 24 hours in refrigerator. Turn occasionally to get full penetration. Lay strips on oven rack & bake at 150 degrees for 4 hours.

Turkey wives are special. They put up with yelps, cutts and cackles year round. They roll out of bed in the middle of the night to send their hunter off full of hot coffee and sometimes breakfast. Then they cheerfully work that kitchen magic that turns a trophy tom into something good to eat. And although they know they are appreciated, they are seldom told so in plain language. Every turkey hunter should take the time to say thanks to his lady. That is small pay for all of those delicious wild turkey dinners.

Hunters work hard in the woods but it is the turkey hunter wives who do the kitchen work.

A LOOK AHEAD
CHAPTER TWENTY-EIGHT

The turkey, both the domestic and wild strains, has had an important impact on North American culture. A roast turkey, sometimes a wild bird but most often one of the broad-breasts or butterballs types, is the main meal for millions on the holiday we call Thanksgiving, the day we set aside to show our appreciation for the bounty received from the woods and the fields. Thanksgiving, much of the time, is referred to as turkey day.

The big bird has earned a place in our music (Turkey in the Straw), in landmark names (notice the abundance of Turkey Mountains, Turkey Knobs, Turkey Buttes and Turkey Creeks), and in the heart of the wild turkey hunter. Spring and fall hunters nationwide flood the economy with millions of hunter dollars. The companies that supply the needs of those who hunt the wild turkey gross many millions more. Money collected from hunters through license fees, Pittman-Robertson funds and direct donations provides millions of dollars for the wise management of this generous renewable resource.

The National Wild Turkey Federation works with state and federal wildlife management agencies. (Photo by Bob Miles, Arizona Game & Fish Dept).

What does the future hold for the wild turkey? To accurately predict the future it is necessary to briefly examine the past.

The original range of the wild turkey, at about the time that the Englanders settled the east coast, covered all or parts of 39 states, the southern tip of Ontario, Canada, and south into Mexico and Central America. The vast flocks of Meleagris gallopavo and the few flocks of Meleagris ocellata were estimated to number nearly ten million. Some modern biologists believe that estimate to be conservative. A history of Montgomery County, Missouri, written in 1830, noted that there were so many wild turkeys that there was no economic reason to consider growing a domesticated variety.

The Indians of Mexico domesticated gallopavo (from Meleagris gallopavo, gallopavo now extinct) at a point in time before the birth of Christ. The birds were about in abundance when the Spaniards "discovered" the new world during the early 1500's. The Spaniards took turkeys to Spain on the return trip and in a relatively short time the big bird was somewhat common in many parts of Europe.

The English who settled the east coast of New England brought some of these travelling turkeys back to their native shores. Even then, if historical records are to be believed, many of these pilgrims preferred the taste of the wild turkey to that of the domesticated strain.

Turkey became a common commodity at pioneer meat markets, some selling for as little as six cents a bird. Market hunters took a terrible toll. The unrestricted hunting, compounded by habitat loss, caused the wild turkey to disappear from much of this historic range by the 1800's. The last half of the 19th century saw the turkey gone or nearly gone from most of it's eastern range. Those were the darkest of days for the wild turkey.

Restoration efforts began about the time that the federal congress passed the Pittman-Robertson Act in 1937. This "hunter tax" made money available for wildlife restoration.

The restoration efforts were pretty much put on hold between 1941 and 1946 because of World War II. Shortly after the war ended, however, state wildlife biologists became serious about re-starting restocking the wild turkey.

Eastern biologists tried the easy route to restocking originally. Pen raised birds, usually a mix of domestic and wild stock, were released into historic habitat. These game farm birds dramatically increased turkey numbers on a short term basis but did nothing to effect a long term increase. To survive in the wild, it turned out, the turkey needed every single one of his wild genes. Those pen raised birds that were released into areas that contained a remnant population of wild turkeys may have caused a decrease in long term turkey numbers. The pen raised hybrids bred with the wild stock to dilute the wild strain. Diseases carried to the wild by the pen raised birds caused a die off.

Some trapped turkeys are fitted with miniaturized transmitters so that biologists are provided an insight into the turkey lifestyle.

The western sub-species, the Rio Grandes and the Merriams, fared better during early restocking efforts. A remnant population of both remained and willingly walked into the open ended traps then in use. Birds were available for restocking. Many Merriams were transported to states without the historic range. A few Merriams were released in Wyoming in 1935. By 1958 the Wyoming flock was estimated to be about 100,000 birds. South Dakota released 29 Merriams into the Black Hills between1948 and 1951. Ten years later the Black Hills flock numbered nearly ten thousand birds.

Restocking efforts in the east were mainly unsuccessful. The Eastern turkey was hesitant to enter the corral type traps used so successfully in the west and it was difficult and time consuming, and therefore expensive, to collect any quantity of birds for transplanting. Finally the perfection of a cannon net trap designed for waterfowl trapping provided the tool needed to capture wild Eastern birds by the bunch.

The perfection of the cannon net provided an efficient and eco-nomical way to trap turkeys for transplanting.
(Photo by Bob Miles, Arizona Game & Fish Dept).

The rest, as they say, is history. Sixteen states permitted turkey hunting in 1952. By 1968 that number nearly doubled. Today, with an estimated turkey population that ranges between two and three million, turkey hunting is allowed in 46 states. Many of those states offer both a spring and a fall season.

Considering all of that, the future appears to be uncommonly bright for North America's greatest game bird. Although the causes of area extirpation were varied, the main cause was market hunting. That type of commercial exploitation is not likely to reoc-cur. A second reason for the tough times was habitat modification or destruction. The trend currently is habitat modification that favors the wild turkey.

A third reason for the dramatic decline in wild turkey numbers had to do with a lack of game management interest, game management funding and game management skills. We now know much about the needs and the nature of the wild turkey. We learn more each year. Miniaturized transmitters placed on free roaming birds are providing a biological insight into the mysterious movements of the wild turkey. Each bit of datum gathered adds to the body of knowledge. That added knowledge permits wildlife managers to fine tune their turkey management programs.

The Merriams turkey was transplanted to non-historic range. (Colorado DOW Photo).

There is even an association dedicated to the welfare and wise use of the wild turkey. The National Wild Turkey Federation (the author is a member) is a group of men and women who work hard on behalf of the wild turkey.

Even though the wild turkey population currently prospers, potential threats are about. Poaching is one such threat. A listing of anti-poaching hot lines appears at the end of this chapter. As a responsible hunter, use the toll free number listed to report the game hogs who steal the resource away from law abiding hunters.

Detrimental habitat modification continues. In the west lumber companies often clear cut vast groves of ponderosa pine, taking out roost trees. Livestock interests lease grazing privileges from federally controlled land and sometimes overgraze to the point that little remains for a wild turkey to eat or drink. Electing politicians who have the inclination and the intestinal fortitude to stand up to these two tax subsidized industries can cause the wild turkey to prosper even more.

The greatest game bird, in all probability, will continue to prosper. Wise game management, positive habitat manipulation and poacher control will cause the wild turkey to maintain present numbers and to increase. Dedicated organizations like the National Wild Turkey Federation, working with state and federal wildlife managers, are another plus. It is likely that all of those efforts will cause the exciting love call of the spring gobbler to cascade through the forest for many years.

ANTI-POACHING HOT LINES

STATE	PROGRAM	TELEPHONE	HOURS
Albama	Game Watch	(800) 272-4263	24
Alaska	Fish & Wildlife Safeguard	(800) 478-3377	24
Arizona	Operation Game Thief	(800) 352-0700	24
Arkansas	STOP (Sportsmen Protect Our Wildlife)	(800) 482-9262	24
California	CALTIP (California Turn In Poachers)	(800) 952-5400	24
Colorado	Operation Game Thief	(800) 332-4155 (800) 295-0164	24 24
Connecticut	Operation TIP (Turn In Poachers)	(800) 842-HELP	24
Delaware	Operation Game Theft	(800) 292-3030	24
Florida	Wildlife Alert	South: (800) 282-8002 N.E.: (800) 343-8105	24
		N.W.: (800) 342-1676 Ctrl: (800) 432-9620 Everglades: (800) 432-2046	
Georgia	Project TIP	(800) 241-4113	24
Hawaii	The Conservation Hot Line	Dial Operator and ask for Enterprise 5469	24
Idaho	CAP (Citizens Against Poaching)	(800) 241-4113	24 M-F
Illinois	TIP (Target Illinois Poaching)	(800) 252-0163	8 a.m.-Mid
Indiana	TIP (Turn In A Poacher)	(800) TIP-IDNR	24
Iowa	TIP	(800) 532-2020	24
Kansas	Game Thief	(800) 228-4263	24
Kentucky	Report A Poacher	(800) 25-ALERT	24
Louisiana	Operation Game Thief	(800) 442-2511	
Maine	Alert Us	(800) 253-7887	24
Maryland	CAP (Catch a Poacher)	(800) 635-8075	24
Massachusetts	RAP (Report All Poachers)	(800) 632-8075	24
Michigan	RAP	(800) 292-7800	24
Minnesota	TIP	(800) 652-9093	24

Mississippi	Report Game Violations	(800) BE-SMART	24
Missouri	Operation Game Thief	(800) 392-1111	24
Montana	TIPMONT	(800) 847-6666	24
Nebraska	Operation Game Thief	(603) 742-7627	M-F 8-5
Nevada	Operation Game Thief	(800) 992-3030	24
New Hampshire	Fish & Game Dispatch	(603) 271-3361	M-F 9-5
		(603) 271-3636	N&WE
New Jersey	Operation Game Thief	(800) 222-0456	M-F 8-5
New Mexico	Operation Game Thief	(800) 432-GAME	24
New York	Law Enforcement Division	(518) 457-5680	8-5
North Carolina	Wildlife Watch	(800) 662-7137	24
North Dakota	RAP	(800) 472-2121	24
Ohio	TIP	(800) POACHER	24
Oklahoma	Operation Game Thief	(800) 521-3719	
			M-F 8-4:30
Oregon	TIP	(800) 452-7888	24
Pennsylvania	Law Enforcement Division	(717) 787-4250	8-4
Rhode Island	General Information Line	(401) 277-2284	24
South Carolina	Operation Game Thief	(800) 592-5522	24
Tennessee	Stop Poaching	(800) 255-8972	24
Texas	Operation Game	(800) 792-GAME	24
Utah	Help Stop Poaching	(800) 662-DEER	24
Vermont	Operation Game Thief	(800) 75-ALERT	24
Virginia	Game Violations	(800) 237-5712	24
Washington	Poaching Hot Line	(800) 562-5626	24
West Virginia	Net Game	(800) NET-GAME	24
Wisconsin	Turn In Poachers	(800) TIP-WDNR	24
Wyoming	Stop Poaching Program	(800) 442-4331	24

Note: The toll-free 800 numbers listed can be dialed only from telephones within each individual state. Also, some states listed as operating a 24-hour hot line use telephone answering machines outside of working hours.

CALL NO POACH INC. TO REPORT ANY POACHING VIOLATION NATIONWIDE (800)227-6224

TURKEY HUNTING SAFETY
CHAPTER TWENTY-NINE

Hide out hunters, those who camo up to sit invisibly to make a noise like a tom turkey's girl friend, place themselves at risk. A very small risk in most instances. Hundreds of thousands of turkey hunters take to the spring and the fall woods each year. Of that total a statistically unimportant number are accidentally shot at, shot at and hit, or shot at, hit, and seriously injured or killed. This point is made, not in an attempt to minimize a very serious problem, but in an effort to place that problem into the proper perspective. Hunters who stay out of the turkey woods because of the danger are missing a lot of recreation because of a small risk.

On the other side of the coin, if you or someone close to you suffers because of the actions of a careless hunter, the statistics become as meaningless as possum poop. Here are techniques the author (and a lot of other good turkey hunters) use to keep their butts safe in the turkey woods.

One turkey hunting risk involves a threat from a hunter you know well, one whose actions you totally control. That hunter, in the event you have not already guessed, is you your own self. The excitement produced by a close encounter of the gobbler kind can cause the most careful hunter to place himself at risk. Some turkey hunting accidents occur when a hunter slams on the brakes and leaps from his vehicle, grabbing for the gun, in an effort to road blast a turkey before it can travel out of gun range. Those road hunters are seldom successful in their attempt to shoot the turkey but sometimes succeed in shooting themselves or a companion.

Other self inflicted injuries can occur when the hunter hurries after a crippled turkey, neglecting to place his gun on safe before he or she begins the race. Other accidents occur during fence crossings, stream crossings or when making a traverse of particularly rough country. All of us know the basics of gun safety. There are times, however, when all of us must concentrate very hard to remember that those basics are important for every second of every hunt.

Some turkey hunting accidents (most, actually) occur when one hunter mistakes another hunter for a turkey. If the target sounds like a turkey, some careless hunters philosophize, then it is a proper target. Adding clothing that somewhat resembles the many colors of a turkey's head or body can compound the danger. You not only sound like a turkey but you even look a little bit like a turkey. Smart hunters stay away from the patriotic colors of a turkeys head, colors like red, white or blue.

Adding a hen decoy to the set up creates even more danger. The fact that the decoy is a hen and the legal spring target is a gobbler does not make decoys more safe. The careless hunter may not care about the sex of the turkey. Or he or she may be the type of hunter who would never knowingly shoot an illegal turkey but may not be able to tell the difference between a hen and a tom. Being shot by a hunter who is dumb hurts just as badly as being shot by a hunter who has a bad attitude.

Stalking a turkey (or a noise that sounds like a turkey) goes against one of the commandments of turkey hunting safety. Too many hunters, unfortunately, do exactly that. If you are on a setup and discover that your sweet clucks and yelps have attracted another hunter do not attempt a friendly wave. The stalker might mistake your hand movement for a turkey head and might impulsively blast away. Do not jump up and try to run. The stalker might immediately recognize that you are not a turkey, but might decide that you are something and that you are about to get away. Getting shot while running away hurts nearly as bad as being shot while sitting.

The best bet, most of the time, is to shout something that is bound to get the stalker's attention. Be as civil as you can, considering your own nature and the circumstances. Try for a statement that is strong enough to indicate your displeasure and concern, but not so insulting that the stalker is outraged, causing him or her to shoot in retaliation.

The following safety suggestions have been compiled by the folks at the National Wild Turkey Federation. The observance of each and every one will do much to keep your body safe while you are in the turkey woods.

* Never stalk a turkey
* Eliminate the colors red, white and blue from your turkey
   hunting outfit.
* Never move, wave or make turkey sounds to alert another hunter
   of your presence.
* Be particularly careful when using a gobbler call.
* When selecting your calling position, don't hide so well that you
   cannot see what's happening.
* Select a calling position that provides a background that totally
   protects your body.
* Never shoot at sounds or movement.
* Be 100% certain of your target (and beyond), before you pull the
   trigger.
* When turkey hunting, assume that every sound you hear is made
   by another hunter.
* When hunting the wild turkey, always think and act defensively.

The National Rifle Association, the organization that works industriously to protect the gun rights of all of us, has compiled a like list, one dealing with the basics of gun handling safety. Much on the list is basic. All of the advice, however, is good advice that can help protect us while on a turkey hunt, or while on any other kind of hunt. Here are the NRA suggestions, paraphrased, from their book Wild Turkey Hunting, (NRA Hunter Skills Series, NRA Sales Department, P.O. Box 96031, Washington DC 20090-6031).

* Keep your gun muzzle pointed in a safe direction.
* Be certain of your target before shouldering your gun.
* If there is any doubt about shooting...don't shoot.
* Be certain the ammunition you load is correct for your gun. Carry only one caliber or gauge, the correct one for the gun you carry.
* If you fall, keep the muzzle pointed in a safe direction. Unload and check the gun for damage or bore obstructions.
* Unload your gun before crossing a fence or traversing hazardous terrain.
* Keep your gun clean and in good condition.
* Know the range of your rifle or shotgun. Be aware that other hunters, non-target animals and property might be in your line of fire.
* Fatigue, excitement and adverse weather conditions can cause mistakes in judgement. Make an effort to "think safety" even under difficult conditions.
* Always be aware of where hunting companions are and control your direction of fire accordingly. Be certain that your hunting companions do the same.
* Booze and drugs do not mix well with gunpowder.
* When the hunt is over unload your gun immediately. Leave the action open for extra safety.
* If your hunting companions are not safety conscious have a talk with them. If they do not improve seek out a new set of hunting companions.

Spring turkey hunting is one of the most exciting of all hunts. The hunter is treated to a wondrous display, both visual and audible, of turkey lust. That enjoyable hunt can be made even more enjoyable if the small worry of hunter safety is minimized. The author wishes you a heap of happy hunts, asks that you call'em in close, and sincerely hopes that each of your trophies will carry paint brush beards and spurs the shape and size of a snickersnee. Good hunting.

APPENDIX

RECOMMENDED READING

Bailey, Wayne: 50 Years Hunting the Wild Turkey, Penn's Woods Products, Inc. 19 West Pittsburgh Street, Delmont, PA 15626. 132 pages. Soft cover.

Bland, Dwain: Turkey Hunter's Digest, DBI Books, 4092 Commercial Avenue, Northbrook, IL 60062. 256 Pages. Soft cover.

Bristol, Stewart J: Hunting Wild Turkeys in New England, North Country Press, Thorndike, Maine. 170 pages. Soft cover.

Brobst, Jack: Bowhunting For Turkeys, R.D. 2, Box 2172, Bangor, PA 18013. 131 pages. Soft cover.

Burnham, Murry: Murry Burnham's Hunting Secrets, Burnham Brothers, P.O. Box 669, Marble Falls, TX 78654. 265 pages. Hard cover.

Camp, Doug: Turkey Hunting Spring and Fall, Outdoor Skills Bookshelf, P.O. Box 111501, Nashville, TN 37211. 165 pages. Soft cover.

Davis, Henry E.: The American Wild Turkey, Old Masters Publishers, Route 2, Box 217, Mdeon, TN 38356. 328 pages. Hard cover. Reprint.

Elliot, Charlie: Field Guide to Wild Turkey Hunting, Penn's Woods Products, 19 West Pittsburgh Street, Delmont, PA 15626. 83 pages.

Eye, Ray: Hunting Wild Turkeys with Ray Eye, Stackpole Books, P.O. Box 1831, Harrisburg, PA 17105. 208 pages. Hard cover.

Fears, J. Wayne: Cooking the Wild Harvest, Stackpole Books, P.O. Box 1831, Harrisburg, PA 17105. 183 pages. Soft cover.

Geurink, Denny: Hunting the Wild Turkey in Michigan, The Michigan Wild Turkey Federation , 20909 Pearl, Farmington Hills, MI 48024. 106 pages. Soft cover.

Harbour, Dave: Advanced Wild Turkey Hunting & World Records, National Wild Turkey Federation, P.O. Box 530, Edgefield, SC 29824. 284 pages. Hard cover.

Jacob, Bart: The Grand Spring Hunt for America's Wild Turkey, Old Jake Products, Pawlet, VT 05761. 194 pages. Hard cover.

Kelly, Tom: The Tenth Legion, Wingfeather Press, P.O. Box 50, Spanish Fort, AL 36527-0050. 119 pages. Hard cover.

McDaniel, John M: Spring Turkey Hunting, The Serious Hunter's Guide, Stackpole Books, P.O. Box 1831, Harrisburg, PA 17105. 219 pages. Hard cover.

McIlhenny, Edward A: The Wild Turkey and It's Huntings. Old Masters Publishers, Route 2, Box 217, Medon, TN 38356. 245 pages. Hard cover. Reprint of 1914 book.

Neill, Robert Hitt: The Flaming Turkey, Mississippi River Publishing, P.O. Box 882, Leland, MS 38756. 178 pages. Hard cover.

Neill, Robert Hitt: The Jakes, Mississippi River Publishing, P.O. Box 882, Leland, MS 38756. 331 pages. Hard cover.

National Rifle Association: Wild Turkey Hunting, NRA Sales Dept, P.O. Box 96031, Washington, D.C. 20090-6031. 182 pages. Soft cover.

Phillips, John E: Outdoor Life-Complete Turkey Hunting, Stackpole Books, P.O. Box 1831, Harrisburg, PA 17105. 318 pages. Hard cover.

Raisch, Roger: Turkey Hunting Secrets, American Heritage Publishers of Iowa, 700 21st Street, West Des Moines, Iowa 50265. 240 pages. Soft cover.

Rue, Leonard Lee III: How I Photograph Wildlife and Nature, Leonard Rue Enterprises, R.D. 3, Box 31, Blairstown, NJ 07825. 287 pages. Hard cover.

Turpin, Tom: Hunting the Wild Turkey, Penn's Woods Products, 19 West Pittsburgh Street, Delmont, PA 15626. 56 pages. Soft cover. Reprint.

Williams, Lovett E. Jr: Studies of the Wild Turkey in Florida, Real Turkeys, 2201 Southeast 41st Avenue, Gainesville, FL 32601. 232 pages. Hard cover.

Williams, Lovett E. Jr: The Art & Science of Wild Turkey Hunting, Real Turkeys, 2201 Southeast 41st Avenue, Gainesville, FL 32601. 331 pages. Hard cover.

Williams, Lovett E. Jr: The Book of the Wild Turkey, Real Turkeys, 2201 Southwest 41st Avenue, Gainesville, FL 32601. 181 pages. Hard cover.

Williams, Lovett E. Jr: The Voice & Vocabulary of the Wild Turkey, Real Turkeys, 2201 Southeash 41st Avenue, Gainesville, FL 32601. 85 pages. Hard cover.

RECOMMENDED VIEWING

<u>Braungardt, Leroy</u>: Bow Hunting The Eastern Wild Turkey, Trophy Hunter Productions (1986). 60 minutes.

<u>Clay, Jim</u>: The Ultimate Turkey Calling Video, Perfection Calls, P.O. Box 164, Stephenson, VA 22656 (703) 667-4608. (1989) 60 minutes.

<u>Cost, Neil (Gobbler)</u>: Makin' Box Calls, Georgia Chapter of NWTF, 1444 Shady Acres, Drive, Dalton, GA 30720. (1987).

<u>Eye, Ray</u>: Eye on the Wild Turkey, Ray Eye Enterprises, P.O. Box 236, Hillsboro, MO 63050. 60 minutes. (1-800-462-5088).

<u>Gauthier, Tim</u>: World of the Wild Turkey, Untamed Wilderness Productions, P.O. Box 37A, Ossineke, MI 49766. 96 minutes.

<u>Griffen, Gary</u>: America's Wild Turkey, Giffen Productions, Rhinebeck, New York 12572. (1990). 50 minutes.

<u>Gulvas, Denny</u>: Fall Turkey Hunting, Spring Gobbler Hunting, and Spring Gobbler Hunting Advanced Techniques, Wildlife Adventures, Rd #3, Box 235-B, Dubois, PA 15801. (814-371-6555).

<u>Harper, Bill</u>: Turkey Hunting, Lohman Manufacturing, P.O. Box 220, Neosho, MO 64850. (1986).

<u>Keck, Rob</u>: Formula For Success: Turkey Hunting, Leisure Time Products, 3M Center, St Paul, MN 55144. (1-800-248-1989 Ext 5830).

<u>Keck, Rob</u>: Understanding the Wild Turkey, Leisure Time Products, 3M Center, St. Paul MN 55144. (1-800-248-1989 Ext 5830).

<u>Kirby, Dick</u>: Callin' & Huntin' Spring Gobblers with Dick Kerby & Friends, Quaker Boy, 5455 Webster Road, Orchard Park, NY 14127. (1-800-544-1600) (1-800-962-3300 in NY). (1987).

<u>Kirby, Dick</u>: In Quest of the Grand Slam, Quaker Boy, 5455 Webster Road, Orchard Park, NY 14127. (1986).

<u>Miranda, Tom</u>: Professional Wild Turkey Hunting with the Experts, Tom Miranda Outdoors, RR 1, Box 10, Chamberlain, SD 57325. (1- 800-356-6730). 60 minutes.

<u>Pittman, Preston</u>: The Double Grand Slam of the American Wild Turkey, Preston Pittman Game Calls, P.O. Box 568, Lucedale, MS 39452. (1-800-446-9941). 120 minutes.

<u>Primos, Wilbur</u>: The Truth About Spring Turkey Hunting, Primos Wild Game Calls, P.O. Box 12785, Jackson, MS 39236. (1-800-523- 2395). 1988

<u>Primos, Wilbur</u>: The Truth II, Primos Wild Game Calls. (1990).

256

LISTING OF NATIONAL FORESTS

NORTHERN REGION

Federal Building
200 East Broadway Street
P.O Box 7669
Missoula, MT 59807
406-329-3511

IDAHO
Clearwater National Forest
12730 Highway 12
Orofino, ID 83544
208-476-4541

Idaho Panhandle National Forests:
Coeur d'Alene, Kaniksu, and
St.Joe National Forests
1201 Ironwood Drive
Coeur d'Alene, ID 83814
208-765-7223

Nez Perce National Forest
East U.S. Highway 13
Route 2, P.O. Box 475
Grangeville, ID 83530
208-983-1950

MONTANA
Beaverhead National Forest
610 North Montana Street
Dillon, MT 59725
406-683-3900

Bitterroot National Forest
316 North Third Street
Hamilton, MT 59840
406-363-3131

Custer National Forest
2602 First Avenue North
Billings, MT 59103
406-657-6361

Deerlodge National Forest
Federal Building
Corner of Cooper and Main
Streets
P.O Box 400
Butte, MT 59703
406-496-3400

Flathead National Forest
1935 Third Avenue East
Kalispell, MT 59901
406-755-5401

Gallatin National Forest
Federal Building
10 East Babcock Street
P.O. Box 130
Bozeman, MT 59771
406-587-6701

Helena National Forest
Federal Building
301 South Park, Room 328
Drawer 10014
Helena, MT 59626
406-449-5201

Kootenai National Forest
506 U.S. Highway 2 West
Libby, MT 59923
406-293-6211

Lewis & Clark National Forest
1101 15th Street North
P.O. Box 871
Great Falls, MT 59403
406-791-7700

Lolo National Forest
Building 24
Fort Missoula
Missoula, MT 59801
406-329-3750

ROCKY MOUNTAIN REGION

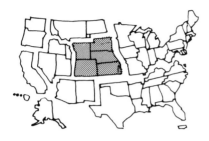

11177 West Eighth Avenue
P.O Box 25127
Lakewood, CO 80225
303-326-9431

COLORADO
Arapaho and Roosevelt National
Forests
240 West Prospect Road
Fort Collins, CO 80526
303-224-1100

Grand Mesa, Uncompahgre, and
Gunnison National Forests
2250 U.S. Highway 50
Delta, CO 81416
303-874-7691

Pike and San Isabel National
Forests
1920 Valley Drive
Pueblo, CO 81008
719-545-8737

Rio Grande National Forest
1803 West U.S. Highway 160
Monte Vista, CO 81144
719-852-5941

Routt National Forest
29587 West U.S. Highway 40
Suite 20
Steamboat Springs, CO 80487
303-879-1722

San Juan National Forest
701 Camino Del Rio
Durango, CO 81301
303-247-4874

White River National Forest
Old Federal Building
Ninth Street and Grand Avenue
P.O. Box 948
Glenwood Springs, CO 81602
303-945-2521

NEBRASKA
Nebraska National Forest
270 Pine Street
Chadron, NE 69337
308-432-3367

SOUTH DAKOTA
Black Hills National Forest
Highway 385 North
Route 2, P.O Box 200
Custer, SD 57730
605-673-2251

WYOMING
Bighorn National Forest
1969 South Sheridan Avenue
Sheridan, WY 82801
307-672-0751

Medicine Bow National Forest
605 Skyline Drive
Laramie, WY 82070
307-745-8971

Shoshone National Forest
225 West Yellowstone Avenue
P.O Box 2140
Cody, WY 82414
307-527-6241

SOUTHWESTERN REGION

Federal Building
517 Gold Avenue SW
Albuquerque, NM 87102
505-842-3292

ARIZONA
Apache-Sitgreaves National Forest
Federal Building
309 South Mountain Avenue
P.O. Box 640
Springerville, AZ 85938
602-333-4301

Coconino National Forest
2323 East Greenlaw Lane
Flagstaff, AZ 86004
602-527-7400

Cornado National Forest
300 West Congress Street
Sixth Floor
Tucson, AZ 85701
602-629-6483

Kaibab National Forest
800 South Sixth Street
Williams, AZ 86046
602-635-2681

Prescott National Forest
344 South Cortez
Prescott, AZ 86303
602-445-1762

Tonto National Forest
2324 East McDowell Road
P.O. Box 5348
Phoenix, AZ 85010
602-225-5200

NEW MEXICO
Carson National Forest
Forest Service Building
208 Criz Alta Road
P.O Box 558
Taos, NM 87571
505-758-6200

Cibola National Forest
10308 Candelaria NE
Albuquerque, NM 87112
505-275-5207

Gila National Forest
2610 North Silver Street
Silver City, NM 88061
505-388-8201

Lincoln National Forest
Federal Building
11th Street and New York
Avenue
Alamogordo, NM 88310
505-437-6030

Santa Fe National Forest
Pinton Building
1220 St. Francis Drive
P.O. Box 1689
Santa Fe, NM 87504
505-988-6940

INTERMOUNTAIN REGION

Federal Building
324 25th Street
Ogden, UT 84401
801-625-5354

IDAHO
Boise National Forest
1750 Front Street
Boise, ID 83702
208-334-1516

Caribou National Forest
Federal Building, Suite 282
250 South Fourth Avenue
Pocatello, ID 83201
208-236-6700

Chalis National Forest
Forest Service Building
U.S. Highway 93 North
P.O. Box 404
Challis, ID 83226
208-879-2285

Payette National Forest
106 West Park Street
P.O Box 1026
McCall, ID 83638
208-634-8151

Salmon National Forest
U.S. Highway 93 North
P.O Box 729
Salmon, ID 83467
208-756-2215

Sawtooth National Forest
2647 Kimberly Road East
Twin Falls, ID 83301
208-737-3200

Targhee National Forest
420 North Bridge Street
P.O Box 208
St. Anthony, ID 83445
208-624-3151

NEVADA
Humboldt National Forest
976 Mountain City Highway
Elko, NV 89801
702-738-5171

Toiyabe National Forest
1200 Franklin Way
Sparks, NV 89431
702-355-5301

UTAH
Ashley National Forest
Ashton Energy Center
355 North Vernal Avenue
Vernal, UT 84078
801-789-1181

Dixie National Forest
82 North 100 East
P.O. Box 580
Cedar City, UT 84720
801-586-2421

Fishlake National Forest
115 East 900 North
Richfield, UT 84701
801-896-4491

Manti-Lasal National Forest
599 West Price River Drive
Price, UT 84501
801-637-2817

Uinta National Forest
88 West 100 North
Provo, UT 84601
801-377-5780

Wasatch-Cache National Forest
8230 Federal Building
125 South State Street
Salt Lake City, UT 84138
801-524-5030

WYOMING
Bridger-Teton National Forest
Forest Service Building
340 North Cache
P.O. Box 1888
Jackson, WY 83001
307-733-2752

PACIFIC SOUTHWEST
REGION

630 Sansome Street
San Francisco, CA 94111
415-556-0122

CALIFORNIA
Angeles National Forest
701 North Santa Anita Avenue
Arcadia, CA 91006
818-574-1613

Cleveland National Forest
880 Front Street
Room 5-N-14
San Diego, CA 92188
619-557-5050

Eldorado National Forest
100 Forni Road
Placerville, CA 95667
916-644-6048

Inyo National Forest
873 North Main Street
Bishop, CA 93514
619-873-5841

Klamath National Forest
1312 Fairlane Road
Yreka, CA 96097
916-842-6131

Lake Tahoe Basin Management
Unit
870 Emerald Bay Road
P.O. Box 731002
South Lake Tahoe, CA 96130
916-573-2600

Lassen National Forest
55 South Sacramento Street
Susanville, CA 96130
916-257-2151

Los Padres National Forest
6144 Calle Real
Goleta, CA 93117
805-683-6711

Mendocino National Forest
420 East Laurel Street
Willows, CA 95988
916-934-3316

Modoc National Forest
441 North Main Street
Alturas, CA 96101
916-233-5811

Plumas National Forest
159 Lawrence Street
P.O. Box 11500
Quincy, CA 95971
916-283-2050

San Bernardino National Forest
1824 South Commercenter Circle
San Bernardino, CA 92408
714-383-5588

Sequoia National Forest
900 West Grand Avenue
Porterville, CA 93257
209-784-1500

Shasta-Trinity National Forests
2400 Washington Avenue
Redding, CA 96001
916-246-5222

Sierra National Forest
1130 O Street, Room 3009
Fresno, CA 93721
209-487-5155

Six Rivers National Forest
507 F Street
Eureka, CA 95501
707-442-1721

Stanislaus National Forest
19777 Greenley Road
Sonora, CA 95370
209-532-3671

Tahoe National Forest
Highway 49 and Coyote Street
Nevada City, CA 95959
916-265-4531

PACIFIC NORTHWEST REGION

319 SW Pine Street
P.O. Box 3623
Portland, OR 97208
503-221-2877

OREGON
Columbia River Gorge National
Scenic Area
Waucoma Center, Suite 200
902 Wasco Avenue
Hood River, OR 97031
503-386-2333

Deschutes National Forest
1645 U.S. Highway 20 East
Bend, OR 97701
503-388-2715

Freemont National Forest
524 North G Street
Lakeview, OR 97630
503-947-2151

Malheur National Forest
139 NE Dayton Street
John Day, OR 97845
503-575-1731

Mount Hood National Forest
2955 NW Division Street
Gresham, OR 97030
503-666-0700

Ochoco National Forest
155 North Court Street
P.O. Box 490
Prineville, OR 97754
503-447-6247

Rogue River National Forest
Federal Building
333 West Eighth Street
P.O. Box 520
Medford, OR 97501
503-776-3600

Siskiyou National Forest
200 NE Greenfield Road
P.O. Box 440
Grants Pass, OR 97526
503-479-5301

Siuslaw National Forest
4077 SW Research Way
Corvallia, OR 97339
503-757-4480

Umatilla National Forest
2517 SW Hailey Avenue
Pendleton, OR 97801
503-276-3811

Umpqua National Forest
2900 NW Stewart Parkway
P.O. Box 1008
Roseburg, OR 97470
503-672-6601

Wallowa-Whitman National
Forest
1550 Dewey Avenue
P.O. Box 907
Baker, OR 97814
503-523-6391

Willamette National Forest
211 East Seventh Avenue
P.O. Box 10607
Eugene, OR 97440
503-687-6521

Winema National Foreat
2819 Dahlia Street
Klamath Falls, OR 97601
503-883-6714

WASHINGTON
Colville National Forest
695 South Main Street
Colville, WA 99114
509-684-3711

Gifford Pinchot National Forest
6926 East Fourth Plain
Boulevard
P.O. Box 8944
Vancouver, WA 98668
206-696-7500

Mount Baker-Snoqualmie
National Forests
1022 First Avenue
Seattle, WA 98104
206-442-5400

Okanogan National Forest
1240 South Second Avenue
P.O. Box 950
Okanogan, WA 98840
509-422-2704

Olympic National Forest
801 Capital Way
P.O. Box 2288
Olympia, WA 98507
206-753-9534

Wenatchee National Forest
301 Yakima Street
P.O. Box 811
Wenatchee, WA 98801
509-662-4335

SOUTHERN REGION

1720 Peachtree Road NW
Atlanta, GA 30367
404-347-4191

ALABAMA
National Forests in Alabama:
William B. Bankhead,
Conecuh,Talladega, and Tuskegee
National Forests
1765 Highland Avenue
Montgomery, AL 36107
205-832-4470

ARKANSAS
Ouachita National Forest
Federal Building
100 Reserve Street
P.O. Box 1270
Hot Springs National Park,
AR 71902
501-321-5202

Ozark-St. Francis National Forest
605 West Main Street
P.O. Box 1008
Russellville, AR 72801
501-968-2354

FLORIDA
National Forests in Florida:
Apalachicola, Ocala, and Osceola
National Forests
USDA Forest Service
227 North Bronough Street,
Suite 4061
Tallahassee, FL 32301
904-681-7265

GEORGIA
Chattahoochee-Oconee National
Forests
508 Oak Street NW
Gainesville, GA 30501
404-536-0541

KENTUCKY
Daniel Boone National Forest
100 Vaught Road
Winchester, KY 40391
606-745-3100

LOUISIANA
Kisatchie National Forest
2500 Shreveport Highway
P.O. Box 5500
Pineville, LA 71360
318-473-7160

MISSISSIPPI
National Forests in Mississsippi:
Bienville, Delta, DeSoto, Holly
Springs, Homochitto, and
Tombigbee National Forests
100 West Capitol Street, Suite 1141
Jackson, MS 39269
601-965-4391

NORTH CAROLINA
National Forests in
North Carolina: Croatan,
Nantahala, Pisgah,and
Uwharrie National Forests
100 Otis Street
P.O. Box 2750
Asherville, NC 28802
704-257-4200

PUERTO RICO AND
THE VIRGIN ISLANDS
Caribbean National Forest
University of Puerto Rico
Agricultural Experiment Station
Call Box 2500
Rio Piedras, PR 00928
809-763-3939

SOUTH CAROLINA
Francis Marion-Sumter National
Forests
1835 Assembly Street
P.O. Box 2227
Columbia, SC 29201
803-765-5222

TENNESSEE
Cherokee National Forest
2800 North Ocoee Street NW
P.O. Box 2010
Cleveland, TN 37320
615-476-9700

TEXAS
National Forests in Texas:
Angelina, Davy Crockett, Sabine,
and Sam Houston National
Forests
Homer Garrison Federal
Building
701 North First Street
Lufkin, TX 75901
409-639-8501

VIRGINIA
George Washington National
Forest
101 North Main Street
P.O. Box 233
Harrison Plaza
Harrisonburg, VA 22801
703-433-2491

Jefferson National Forest
210 Franklin Road SW
Roanoke, VA 24001
703-982-6270

ALASKA REGION

Federal Office Building
709 West Ninth Street
P.O. Box 21628
Juneau, AK 99802
907-586-8863

ALASKA
Chugach National Forest
201 East Ninth Avenue, Suite 206
Anchorage, AK 99501
907-271-2500

Tongass National Forest:
Chatham Area
204 Siginaka Way
Sitka, AK 99835
907-747-6671

Ketchikan Area
Federal Building
Ketchikan, AK 99901
907-225-3101

Sitkine Area
201 12th Street
P.O. Box 309
Petersburg, AK 99833
907-772-3841

EASTERN REGION

310 West Wisconsin Avenue,
Room 500
Milwaukee, WI 53202
414-291-6671

ILLINOIS
Shawnee National Forest
901 South Commercial Street
Harrisburg, IL 62946
618-253-7114

INDIANA AND OHIO
Wayne-Hoosir National Forests
811 Constitution Avenue
Bedford, IN 47421
812-275-5987

MICHIGAN
Hiawatha National Forest
2727 North Lincoln Road
Escanaba, MI 49829
906-786-4062

Huron-Manistee National
Forests
421 South Mitchell Street
Cadillac, MI 49601
616-775-2421

Ottawa National Forest
East U.S. Highway 2
Ironwood, MI 49938
906-932-1330

MINNESOTA
Chippewa National Forest
Route 3, P.O. Box 244
Cass Lake, MN 56633
218-335-2226

Superior National Forest
515 West First Street
P.O. Box 338
Duluth, MN 55801
218-720-5324

MISSOURI
Mark Twain National Forest
401 Fairgrounds Road
Rolla, MO 65401
314-364-4621

NEW HAMPSHIRE AND MAINE
White Mountain National Forest
Federal Building
719 North Main Street
P.O. Box 638
Laconia, NH 03247
603-524-6450

PENNSYLVANIA
Allegheny National Forest
Spiridon Building
222 Liberty Street
P.O. Box 847
Warren, PA 16365
814-723-5150

VERMONT
Green Mountain and Finger Lakes
National Forests
Federal Building
151 West Street
P.O. Box 519
Rutland, VT 05701
802-773-0300

WEST VIRGINIA
Monongahela National Forest
USDA Building
200 Sycamore Street
Elkins, WV 26241
304-636-1800

WISCONSIN
Chequamegon National Forest
1170 Fourth Avenue South
Park Falls, WI 54552
715-762-2461

Nicolet National Forest
Federal Building
68 South Stevens Street
Rhinelander, WI 54501
715-362-3415

WHERE TO WRITE OR CALL FOR TRAVEL INFORMATION

United States

Alabama Bureau of Tourism & Travel, 532 South Perry St., Montgomery, AL 36104-4614; 800-392-8096, out of state 800-ALABAMA

Alaska Division of Tourism, Box E, Juneau, AK 99811; 907-465-2010

Arizona Office of Tourism, 1480 E. Bethany Home Road, Suite 180, Phoenix, AZ 85014; 602-942-3618

Arkansas Tourism Office, One Capitol Mall, Little Rock, AR 72201; 800-482-8999, out of state 800-643-8383

California Office of Tourism, P.O. Box 189, Sacramento, CA 95812; 800-TO-CALIF

Colorado Tourism Board, 1625 Broadway, Suite 1700, Denver, CO 80202; 800-433-2656, out of state 303-592-5410

Connecticut Dept. of Economic Development, Tourism Division, 210 Washington St., Hartford, CT 06106; 800-842-7492, out of state (ME to VA) 800-243-1685

Delaware Tourism Office, 99 Kings Hwy., Box 1401, Dover, DE 19903; 800-282-8667, out of state 800-441-8846

Florida Division of Tourism, 126 Van Buren St., Tallahassee, FL 32301; 904-487-1462

Georgia Dept. of Industry & Trade, Tourist Division, Box 1776, Atlanta, GA 30301; 404-656-3590

Hawaii Visitors Bureau, Box 8527, Honolulu, HI 96830; 808-923-1811

Idaho Travel Council, Statehouse Mall, 700 W. State St., Boise, ID 83720; 208-334-2470, out of state 800-635-7820

Illinois Tourist Information Center, 310 S. Michigan, Suite 108, Chicago, IL 60604; 800-223-0121

Indiana Dept. of Commerce, Tourism Development Division, One North Capitol, Suite 700, Indianapolis, IN 46204; 800-2-WANDER

Iowa Dept. of Economic Development, Tourism/Film Office, 200 E. Grand, Box 6127, Des Moines, IA 50309; 800-345-IOWA

Kansas Travel & Tourism Division, 400 S.W. 8th, 5th Fl., Topeka, KS 66603; 913-296-2009

Kentucky Dept. of Travel Development, 2200 Capitol Plaza Tower, Frankfort, KY 40601; U.S. & parts of Canada; 800-225-TRIP

Louisiana Office of Tourism, Inquiry Dept., Box 94291, Baton Rouge, LA 70804-9291; 504-342-8119, out of state 800-33-GUMBO

Maine Division of Tourism, Maine Publicity Bureau, 97 Winthrop St., Hallowell, ME 04347-2300; Sept.-April, East Coast U.S. 800-533-9595

Maryland Office of Tourist Development, 217 Redwood St., Baltimore, MD 21202; 800-331-1750, operator 250

Massachusetts Division of Tourism, 100 Cambridge St., 13th Fl., Boston, MA 02202; 617-727-3201 or -3202

Michigan Travel Bureau, Box 30226, Lansing, MI 48909; 800-5432-YES

Minnesota Office of Tourism, 275 Jackson St., 250 Skyway Level, St. Paul, MN 55101; 800-652-9747, out of state 800-328-1461

Mississippi Division of Tourism, 22825, Jackson, MS 39205; 800-647-2290

Missouri Division of Tourism, Box 1055, Jefferson City, MO 65102; 314-751-4133

Montana Promotion Division, 1424 9th Ave., Helena, MT 59620; 406-444-2654, out of state 800-541-1447

Nebraska Division of Travel & Tourism, Box 94666, Lincoln, NE 68509; 800-742-7595, out of state 800-228-4307

Nevada Commission on Tourism, State Capitol Complex, Carson City, NV 89710; 702-885-3636, out of state 800-237-0774

New Hampshire Office of Vacation Travel, 105 Loudon Rd., Box 856, Concord, NH 03301; 603-271-2665, New England Region 800-258-3608

New Jersey Division of Travel & Tourism, One West State St., CN 826, Trenton, NJ 08625; 800-JERSEY-7

New Mexico Tourism & Travel Division, Joseph M. Montoya Bld., 1100 St. Francis Dr., Santa Fe, NM 87503; 800-545-2040

New York State Division of Tourism, One Commerce Plaza, Albany, NY 12245; 800-CALL NYS

North Carolina Travel & Tourism Division, 430 N. Salisbury St., Raleigh, NC 27611; 800-VISIT NC

North Dakota Tourism Office, Libery Memorial Bldg., Capitol Grounds, Bismarck, ND 58505; 800-472-2100, out of state 800-437-2077

Ohio Divisiion of Travel & Tourism, Box 1001, Columbus, OH 43266; 800-BUCKEYE

Oklahoma Tourism & Recreation Dept., Marketing Services Division, 500 Will Rogers Bldg., Oklahoma City, OK 73105; 800-652-6552

Oregon Economic Development Dept., Tourism Division, 595 Cottage St., NE, Salem, OR 97310; 503-373-1270, out of state 800-547-7482

Pennsylvania Bureau of Travel Development, 416 Forum Bldg., Dept. PR, Harrisburg, PA 17120; 800-VISIT PA, ext. 275

Rhode Island Dept. of Economic Development, Tourism & Promotion Division, 7 Jackson Walkway, Providence, RI 02903; 401-277-2601,ME-VA & N. Ohio 800-556-2484

South Carolina Division of Tourism, 1018 Ferfuson St., Columbia, SC 29202; 803-734-0122

South Dakota Dept. of Tourism, Capitol Lake Plaza, 711 Wells Ave., Pierre, SD 57501; 800-952-2217, out of state 800-843-1930

Tennessee Dept. of Tourism Development, Box 23170, Nashville, TN 37202; 615-741-2158

Tourist Division, Texas Dept. of Commerce, Box 12008, Austin, TX 78711; 512-462-9191

Utah Travel Council, Division of Travel Development, Council Hall/Capitol Hill, Salt Lake City, UT 84114; 801-538-1030

Vermont Travel Division, 134 State St., Montpelier, VT 05602; 802-828-3236

Virginia Division of Tourism, 202 N. 9th St., Suite 500, Richmond, VA 23219; 800-VISIT VA

Washington State Tourism, Development Division, 101 General Administration Bldg., MS AX-13, Olympia, WA 98504; 206-586-2088 or 800-544-1800

Washington, D.C., Convention & Visitors Assoc., 1212 New York Ave. N.W., Suite 600, Washington, D.C., 20005, 202-789-7000

West Virginia Dept. of Commerce, Marketing/Tourism Division, 2101 Washington St., E., 3rd Fl., Charleston, WV 25305; 800-CALL WVA

Wisconsin Division of Tourism Development, 123 W., Washington Ave., Madison, WI 53707; 608-266-2147 or in adjoining states 800-ESCAPES

Wyoming Travel Commission, I-25 and College Dr., Cheyenne, WY 82002; 307-777-7777, out of state 800-225-5996

GENERAL INFORMATION

National Park Service, U.S. Dept. of the Interior, Box 37127, Washington, D.C., 20013; Information 202-343-7394

Forest Service, U.S. Dept. of Agriculture, Box 96090, Washington, D.C., 20090; 202-447-3957

CANADA

Canadian Government Office of Tourism, 235 Queen St., Ottawa, Ontario, Canada K1A 0H6 613-954-3852

Travel Alberta, Box 2500, Edmonton, Alberta, Canada T5J 2Z4; 800-222-6501, in U.S. & Canada 800-661-8888

British Columbia Ministry of Tourism, 1117 Wharf St., Victoria, British Columbia, Canada V8W 2Z2; 604-387-1642 or 800-663-6000

Travel Manitoba, Winnipeg, Manitoba, Canada R3C 3H8; in U.S. & Canada 800-665-0040

New Brunswick Dept. of Tourism, Box 12345, Fredericton, New Brunswick, Canada E3B 5C3; 800-442-4442, in U.S. & Canada 800-561-0123

Newfoundland & Labrador Tourist Services Division, Box 2016, St. John's, Newfoundland, Canada, A1C 5R8; 709-576-2830 or 800-563-NFLD

Northwest Territories Travel Arctic, Yellowknife, Northwest Territories, Canada X1A 2L9; 403-873-7200

Nova Scotia Dept. of Tourism and Culture, Box 130, Halifax, Nova Scotia, Canada B3J 2M7; 902-424-5000; in U.S. 800-341-6096, in ME 800-492-0643

Ontario Travel, Queen's Park, Toronto, Ontario, Canada M7A 2E5; 416-965-4008, U.S. & Canada 800-268-3735

Prince Edward Island Tourism & Parks, Box 940, Charlottestown, Prince Edward Island, Canada C1A 7N8; 902-892-7411

Tourisme Quebec, C.P. 20,000, Quebec, QC, Canada G1K 7X2; 800-361-5405, in Ontario & Maritimes 800-361-6490, in eastern U.S. except FL 800-443-7000

Tourism Saskatchewan, 1919 Saskatchewan Dr., Regina, Saskatchewan, Canada S4P 3V7; In Saskatchewan, 800-667-7538, in U.S. & Canada 800-667-7191

Yukon Territory, Tourism Yukon CG, Box 2703, Whitehorse, Yukon Territory, Canada Y1A 2C6; 403-667-5338

MEXICO

Mexican Government Tourism Office, 405 Park Ave., New York, N.Y., 10022; 212-838-2949

274

MANUFACTURERS' WARRANTY CENTERS

Action Arms
1120 Orthodox St.
Philadelphia, PA 19124
1-215-739-6400

Aimpoint USA
203 Elden St., Suite 302
Herndon, VA 22070
1-800-336-1085

American Arms, Inc.
715 East Armour Rd.
North Kansas City, MO 64116
1-816-474-3161

American Industries
8700 Brookport Rd.
Cleveland, OH 46129
1-216-398-8300

Arcadia Machine
536 N. Vincent Ave.
Covina, CA 91722
1-818-915-7803

Barnett International
1967 Gunn Highway
Odessa, FL 33556
1-800-237-4507

Bear Archery
RR 4-4600 SW 41st Blvd.
Gainsville, FL 32601
1-800-874-2327

Beeman Inc.
47 Paul Dr.
San Rafael, CA 94903
1-415-472-7121

Beretta Arms
17801 Indian Head Hwy.
Accokeek, MD 20607
1-301-283-2191

Bersa Inc.
967 Watertower Ln.
Dayton, OH 45449
1-800-843-OSHI

Browning Co.
624-B Tenbrook Rd.
Arnold, MO 63010
1-800-453-2349

Charter Arms
430 Sniffens Lane
Stratford, CT 06497
1-203-377-8080

Colt Ind.
25 Talcott Rd.
W. Hartford, CT 06110
1-203-236-6311

Crosman Co.
980 Turk Hill Rd.
Fairport, NY 14450
1-716-223-6000

C.V.A.
P.O. Box 1528
Norcross, GA 30091
1-404-449-4687

Daisy Manufacturing Co.
Service Dept. #2, Box 220
Rogers, AR 72756
1-800-643-3458

Darton Archery
3540 Darton Rd.
Hale, MI 48739
1-313-239-7361

Nynamit Nobel
105 Stonehurst Ct.
Northvale, NJ 07647
1-201-767-1660

Excam Co.
4480 E. 11th Ave.
Hialeah, FL 33013
1-305-681-4461

Federal Ordnance
1443 Potrero Ave. South
El Monte, Ca 91733
1-800-327-7487

F.I.E.
4541 N.W. 133rd St.
Opa-Locka, FL 33054
1-800-327-7487

Glock Co.
Suite 190
5000 Highlands Pkwy.
Smyrna, GA 30080
1-205-655-3352

Golden Eagle
104 S. Mill St.
Creswell, OR 97426
1-800-336-2212

Indian Archery
817 Maxwell Ave.
Evansville, IN 47717
1-800-457-3373

Interarms Co.
10 Prince St.
Alexandria, VA 22313
1-703-548-1400

K.W. Caplight
3555 Howard St.
Skokie, IL 60076
1-312-982-9069

Lee Precision
4275 Highway U.
Hartford, WI 53027
1-414-673-3075

Leupold Co.
600 N.W. Meadow Dr.
Beaverton, OR 97006
1-503-646-9171

Lyman Co.
Route 147
Middlefield, CT 06455
1-203-349-3421

Mag-Lite
1635 So. Sacramento Ave.
Ontario, CA 91761
1-714-947-1006

Marlin Arms
100 Kenna Dr.
N. Haven, CT 06473
1-203-239-5621

Mayville Engineering
715 South St.
Mayville, WI 53050
1-414-387-4500

Mossberg
7 Grasso Ave.
New Haven, CT 06473
1-203-2880-6491

Moultree Feeders
2113 Southwood Rd.
Birmingham, AL 35216
1-205-823-2117

New England Firearms
Co., Inc.
Industrial Row
Gardner, MA 01440
1-617-632-9393

Onieda Eagle
235 Cortland Ave.
Syracuse, NY 13202
1-315-474-1876

Pacific Tool Co.
3625 Old Potash Hwy.
Grand Island, NE 68803
1-308-384-2308

Pioneer (Steiner) Co.
Bjorn Harms
216 Haddon Ave. Suite 522
Westmont, NJ 08108
1-800-257-7742

Ranging Co.
Route 5 & 20
East Bloomfield, NY 14443
1-800-828-1495

R.C.B.S. Inc.
Scales: OHaus Scale Corp.
29 Hanover Rd.
Florham Park, NJ 07932
Other: OMark Repair
605 Oro Dam Blvd.
Oroville, CA 95965
1-800-635-2050

Redfield Co.
5800 East Jewell Ave.
Denver, CO 80224
1-303-757-6411

Remington Arms
Arms Service Div.
Ilioin, NY 13357
1-302-773-5292

Savage Ind.
330 Lockhouse Rd.
Westfield, MA 01085
1-413-562-2361

Simmons
14205 S.W. 119 Ave.
Miami, FL 33186
1-305-252-0477

Sturm, Ruger Co.
Sing. Act. Rev., Semi-Aut. Pist.
& 44 Car.
10 Lacey Place
Southport, CT 06490
1-203-259-4843

Shotguns, Rifles & Dbl. Act.
Revolvers
Guild Road
Newport, NH 03773
1-603-863-3300

Tasco Inc.
7600 N.W. 26th St.
Miami, FL 33122
1-305-591-3670

Thompson Center Arms
Farmington Rd.
Rochester, NH 03867
1-603-332-2427

Trius Co.
Box 25
Cleves, OH 45002
1-513-941-5682

U.S. Repeating Arms
275 Winchester Ave.
New Haven, CT 06535
1-203-789-5000

U.S. Sporting Products
Hwy. 311
Spring Branch, TX 78070
1-512-885-4203

York Co.
P.O. Box 110
Independence, MO 64051
1-816-252-9612

The Forest Service

United States Department of Agriculture

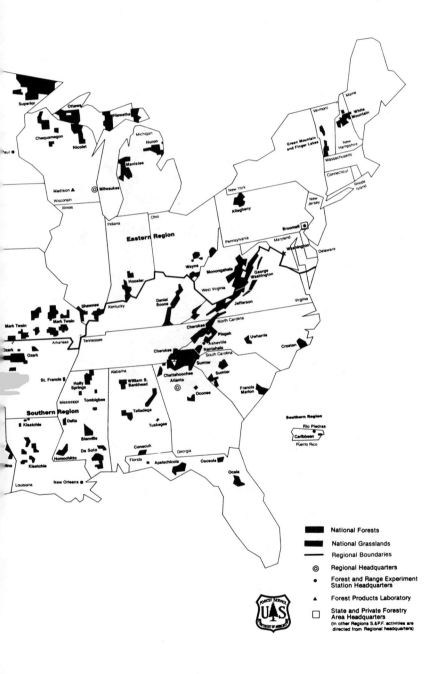

National Forests
National Grasslands
Regional Boundaries
◎ Regional Headquarters
• Forest and Range Experiment Station Headquarters
▲ Forest Products Laboratory
□ State and Private Forestry Area Headquarters
(In other Regions S.&P.F. activities are directed from Regional headquarters)

279